MAKING IT IN
PUBLIC RELATIONS

MAKING IT IN

Public Relations

AN INSIDER'S GUIDE TO CAREER OPPORTUNITIES

Leonard Mogel

COLLIER BOOKS
MACMILLAN PUBLISHING COMPANY
NEW YORK

MAXWELL MACMILLAN CANADA
TORONTO

MAXWELL MACMILLAN INTERNATIONAL
NEW YORK   OXFORD   SINGAPORE   SYDNEY

Collier Books
Macmillan Publishing Company
866 Third Avenue
New York, NY 10022

Maxwell Macmillan Canada, Inc.
1200 Eglinton Avenue East
Suite 200
Don Mills, Ontario M3C 3N1

Macmillan Publishing Company is part of the Maxwell Communication
Group of Companies.

LIBRARY OF CONGRESS CATALOGING-IN-PUBLICATION DATA
Mogel, Leonard.
Making it in public relations / Leonard Mogel.—1st Collier Books ed.
p.   cm.
ISBN 0-02-070180-2
1. Public relations—United States.   I. Title.
HM263.M59   1993   92-27334
659.2—dc20

Macmillan books are available at special discounts for bulk purchases for sales
promotions, premiums, fund-raising, or educational use. For details, contact:

Special Sales Director
Macmillan Publishing Company
866 Third Avenue
New York, NY 10022

First Collier Books Edition 1993

10 9 8 7 6 5 4 3 2 1

Printed in the United States of America

To my loving daughters, Wendy Lynn Mogel and Jane Ellen Mogel, for bringing joy into my life.

CONTENTS

PART III A CLOSER LOOK AT THE COMPONENTS
OF PUBLIC RELATIONS

PART IV PURSUING A CAREER IN PUBLIC RELATIONS

ACKNOWLEDGMENTS

Appreciation goes to my wife and best friend, Ann Mogel. We did it again. What more can I say?

My sincere thanks goes to my editor, Natalie Chapman, for her professional excellence, guidance, and intelligent advice. She brought the keenest of critical eyes to bear on this book as she has on *Making It in Advertising*. Thanks, too, to Nancy Cooperman for her cheerful cooperation.

I wish to thank all the people who enhanced this book by agreeing to be interviewed: Howard Rubenstein, Daniel Maier, John West, Madalene Milano, and Brigitte Devine.

I may miss a few names, but my sincere appreciation for splendid cooperation goes to Donna Peltier and Colleen McDonough of PRSA; Donna Erickson of the Institute for PR Research and Education; Jim Sinkinson of the *Bulldog Reporter;* Jim Broadwater of the *Washington Journalism Review;* Cindy Reagan of Ruder Finn; Carla Brock of the American Medical Association; Roger Campbell of the American Heart Association; Peter Thonis of IBM; David Y. Jacobson and Nicholas J. Tortorello of Research & Forecasts; and Susan Fry of the *Public Relations Journal.*

INTRODUCTION

It was a stifling August day. I was a novice printing salesman canvassing the famous Brill Building in New York's Times Square district for prospective customers. The painted metal door of the office had a dozen names listed, so I thought it had good business possibilities. Upon entering, I presented my card to the only person in the office, a slovenly character in his early thirties. He introduced himself as Richie Roberts (his name has been changed for the purpose of this book).

He was on his way out and asked if I would join him for a drink. It was early in the day, but I figured this was a good way to become fast friends, especially if he paid. The drink turned out to be an egg cream, a New York delicacy made of seltzer, chocolate syrup, and milk (no egg). He ordered two for himself and one for me, then walked directly across the street to another candy store where he repeated the order.

Later, back in his office, Roberts told me that he was a press agent. I didn't know just what a press agent did, but I was nonetheless impressed. He went on to explain with pride that most of his clients were Broadway restaurants. His job was to get the names of the restaurants into the major syndicated newspaper gossip columns. To accomplish this, Roberts would "package" a press release that included a small joke attributed to a name comedian or actor who was dining at one of Roberts's client restaurants. All parties benefited from this collaborative "public relations." Columnists were pleased because this kind of journalism required little effort on their part. The comedian got his name in print, and Roberts's restaurant assumed status as the home base of the celebrated. Who could resist eating at Major's Cabin Grill if Phil Silvers or Sid Caesar might be at the next table telling brilliantly funny stories? For this press agentry, Roberts was paid a small amount of cash plus free meals at the restaurant on Monday nights.

Roberts's largest client was a matchmaking service owned by one Sarah Kane; her Roberts-created slogan was "Don't live in vain, see Sarah Kane." For $25 the client was guaranteed three introductions, usually from a roster of unemployed actors. If the client was an older woman, Roberts's father was invariably one of the introductions.

Roberts's career path eventually led him to dubious Hollywood fame as a successful producer and director of "B" movies.

Richie Roberts's brand of PR bears only a remote resemblance to the profession as it exists today. In this book we will discuss the modern practice of PR and how it serves a wide variety of institutions in our society.

PART I

Introduction to
Public Relations

CHAPTER 1

A Short History
of Public Relations

It is said that public relations goes back more than 2,000 years to
the time of Julius Caesar. Caesar may have been recording history
when he wrote his commentaries, but as the leader of all the
Romans he was at the same time persuading the citizens that he was
doing a great job.

Public relations in its most basic form developed in the United
States in the early nineteenth century when newspapers ran friendly
notices in news columns to reward advertisers with "free publicity."
Literary bureaus were developed to contrive such items, and by the
early twentieth century publicity agents, often former journalists,
abounded in New York and in other large cities. This activity was an
important element in the evolution of public relations and continues
in modern-day press agentry and the promotion of special events.

The latter part of the nineteenth century saw the rise of the "robber
barons," industrialists whose grasping, acquisitive business practices
had as their precept "The public be damned." The excesses of these
businessmen were targeted by a group of writers known as "muck-

rakers"—Lincoln Steffens, Upton Sinclair, and Ida Tarbell. To combat the opprobrium heaped on big business by these writers and by an increasingly inquisitive press, the industrialists hired publicists to soften public opinion and cast a more benign light on their activities.

In 1906 Ivy Lee, a former newspaperman and the founder of modern PR, was hired as publicity adviser by a group of U.S. anthracite coal-mine operators who had drawn the attention of the press by their haughty attitudes toward the miners and the press in labor disputes. At that time it was not a common practice for industrialists such as the mine owners to answer questions from the press about their activities. Lee, reasoning that it was good business for the mine operators to be more open, sent out an announcement that the operators would supply the press with all possible information.

Later that year Lee was retained by the Pennsylvania Railroad and introduced a new practice to that industry—the supplying of full information to the press about railroad accidents. In this he was forging a major ingredient of what would later be called public relations.

Much of Ivy Lee's focus was on the oil magnate John D. Rockefeller, who epitomized the robber baron chronicled by Tarbell and her fellow muckrakers. Rockefeller's well-publicized practice of distributing dimes to children was characterized by some reformers as a public relations creation of Ivy Lee's in his efforts to humanize Rockefeller.

Government agencies began hiring publicity experts in Great Britain and the United States early in the twentieth century. These experts were often called "directors of information."

After World War I, public relations came into wide use in business and industry as well as in government. Today, under various titles, all government agencies have public affairs or public relations departments. When an important announcement is made, or a press conference is called, it emanates from these departments.

Significant in the history of modern PR is the contribution of Edward L. Bernays, who in 1992 at the age of 101 is still pursuing an active career. Bernays coined the phrase "counsel on public relations."

This visionary imagemaker is credited with dreaming up the industry of public relations. He wrote the first book and taught the first university course on the subject. His stunts are legendary. When it was taboo for women in the 1920s to smoke cigarettes in public, Bernays had socialites light up "torches of freedom" on Fifth Avenue—and alerted the press.

During his lengthy career, Bernays has counseled such clients as Thomas Edison, Henry Ford, and Eleanor Roosevelt. He also advised former Presidents Woodrow Wilson, Calvin Coolidge, and Dwight D. Eisenhower. Bernays reportedly turned down Adolf Hitler as a client, claiming, "I wouldn't want it on my superego [Bernays's uncle was Sigmund Freud] that I did for money what I wouldn't do without money."

Today, Bernays's "counsel on public relations" has given rise to more than 2,000 PR firms that deal with the interests of their trade and charitable associations and corporate, governmental, and individual clients.

Public relations is a major industry employing more than 200,000 skilled communicators charged with the responsibility of interpreting the client to the public and vice versa.

CHAPTER 2

PR: What It Is, What It Does

Hill and Knowlton is one of the world's premier public relations firms. In recent years it has provided crisis communications counsel for the Three Mile Island nuclear reactor crisis, the Mexico City earthquake, the largest bank insolvency in the world, and the largest industrial bankruptcy.

During the same period, Hill and Knowlton put its skills to work in communications management for Humana's artificial-heart implants, Pope John Paul II's visit to the United States, Harvard University's 350th anniversary, and the 1986 Reagan–Gorbachev summit in Iceland.

While all this was going on, the firm was involved in new-product launches for Crest toothpaste, NutraSweet artificial sweetener, and Discover credit card. It also created new corporate identities for Navistar, Dart & Kraft, and a major international bank.

But that's not all. Hill and Knowlton was active on other fronts. It was the firm's job to tell millions of parents and thousands of store managers that certain pediatric vitamins—an inventory with a market value of $270 million—must be replaced or discarded because of suspected tampering with the packages.

When the U.S. Food and Drug Administration questioned the popular arthritic analgesic of a pharmaceutical agent, Hill and Knowlton confined the issue to scientific questions and prepared materials based on pharmacological evidence and clinical trials. The result: The FDA was satisfied with a minor reformulation, and pharmacists and the public were reassured of the manufacturer's medical integrity.

WHAT IS PUBLIC RELATIONS?

The foregoing are examples of PR in action. We'll discuss many more in this section. But first, some general definitions, beginning with "public relations." A simple definition we like comes from *Lesly's PR Handbook*.[1] PR can be defined as "helping an organization (or group) and its publics adapt mutually to each other."

What is a "public"? A public is an entity *whose attention is sought* by a business corporation, an individual, a performer or writer or artist, a government or governmental agency, a charitable institution, a religious body, or almost any person or organization. The publics may be as diverse as female voters of a particular political party or the shareholders of a public corporation. To the Merck pharmaceutical company, marketing a new anti-depressant drug, its publics are medical practitioners, consumer advocates, the FDA, and, of course, patients.

The concerns of PR deal with the subject entity, or client, and the publics involved. Acquainting the clients with public perceptions of that client is an important element of PR; so is affecting these perceptions by focusing, curtailing, amplifying, or augmenting information about the client as it is conveyed to the publics.

In its simplest form, PR is concerned with creating a favorable climate for marketing the client's products or services. This becomes less simple in a crisis when the client is, say, a public company that shows a large earnings loss for the year or a nuclear energy plant facing a disaster such as the one that occurred at Three Mile Island in 1979.

To a large extent, the job of PR is to make good news as effective as possible and to forestall bad news. When disaster strikes, the PR practitioner's job is to assess the situation and the damage quickly, to assemble all the facts and background information, and to offer these to the news media, along with answers to their questions. It is the responsibility of PR to organize the client's response, often involving complicated issues.

Crisis communications and crisis management are the big-league games of PR. Most other day-to-day activities offer less challenge to the practitioner. Yet they all fit under the umbrella of public relations. We'll see how it unfolds.

The Tools of PR

In carrying out the PR function, the industry calls on many peripheral services. A recent Public Relations Society of America (PRSA) conference in New York showcased a number of these "PR tools." Among these were worldwide press release services, satellite message-delivery systems, video news release preparation, media monitoring, speakers' bureaus, media directories, clipping bureaus, computer-aided research and media analysis, satellite interview tours, desktop publishing, public-speaking training, film and video productions, and databank services.

The sophistication of public relations practice today demands the implementation of these tools in a field in which a PR professional may be called on to perform such diverse activities as producing a thirty-minute promotional film for a client, arranging a speaking tour for a corporation's CEO, or publicizing the introduction of a break-through drug.

The Size of the PR Work Force

According to the most recent report of the U.S. Bureau of Labor Statistics, there are 159,000 PR professionals in the United States. The Institute for PR Research and Education estimates that there are approximately 250,000 to 300,000 people employed in PR and public affairs. John Budd, a prominent executive with a PR firm, claims that there are "some half million people with PR of some sort in their job titles."[2] Whoever is right about the employment numbers, on the basis of the several billion dollars spent annually on PR alone we can conclude that it is a major communications area. It is also one with exciting job possibilities.

Academically, the number of college students majoring in PR has risen dramatically. In the 1960s, only a few colleges offered PR courses. Today, more than 22,000 students at some 300 colleges are either majoring in PR or taking at least one course in this subject.

THE FUNCTIONS OF A PR SPECIALIST

Whether one works for a corporation, an organization, or a PR counsel firm, one will find that various jobs and services are common to all. Following are just a few of the functions of a PR practitioner.

- coordinates media relations for the organization and its divisions;
- plans and implements the organization's PR, public service, and public interest programs;
- writes speeches for executives;
- writes press releases for the trade and consumer press;
- arranges speakers, meetings, and events;
- writes and edits house publications, newsletters, and employee communications;
- acts as spokesperson for organizations in event of accident or disaster;
- arranges press conferences;
- supervises audio/visual materials for sales meetings and financial presentations;
- accompanies CEO and top management on business tours to arrange conventions;
- works with financial staff on presentation of annual and quarterly reports.

PR Counsel Firms

The PR function is carried out at two levels. At a corporation, organization, trade association, or governmental agency, PR is the responsibility of a group of specialists. As we will see in a later chapter, a large corporation such as IBM has a huge staff performing numerous PR and public affairs activities. In addition, many large corporations and organizations supplement their own efforts by retaining outside specialists, called PR counsel. In the industry, counsel organizations are also known as PR counsel firms, PR agencies, PR firms, and agencies.

New York City, the hub of the nation's PR business, is home to hundreds of PR counsel firms. Although these firms do not employ large numbers of people as do advertising agencies, they are nonetheless important adjuncts to their clients' PR programs in the areas of managing crises, establishing global communications, positioning products and brands, and planning special events. We discuss these and other PR counsel firm pursuits in detail in Chapter 4.

Of New York's largest PR counsel firms, 13 employ 100 or more people.[3] The largest PR firm, Burson-Marsteller, a branch of the giant Young & Rubicam advertising agency, employs about 550 people in its New York office to service its 360 clients.

PR counsel firms usually bill their clients on monthly retainers at fees ranging from a low of $1,000 up to $10,000 or more. Occasionally, the firms will perform prescribed services for an agreed-upon fee but will undertake other assignments on a per-project basis.

Account executives at these firms are trained to juggle a number of accounts at the same time. A well-known New York firm, Howard J. Rubenstein Associates, has 122 employees servicing more than 350 clients, including the very active Rupert Murdoch and Donald Trump. At this ratio of employee to clients, Rubenstein's people don't have many coffee breaks.

A trend in recent years has been for advertising agencies to own PR counsel firms—in a sense, being responsible for a client's total communications package. Five out of the top six of New York's largest PR counsel firms are owned by large advertising agency organizations. These large PR firms maintain offices in other U.S. cities and abroad.

THE DIFFERENCE BETWEEN ADVERTISING AND PR

Advertising and PR are related, but there are definite differences. Advertising involves the planning, creation, and placement of sales messages for products and services. PR is concerned with corporate, financial, and marketing communications; product publicity; and public affairs. An ad agency will create TV and print ads for Kraft's margarine. Kraft's PR firm will publicize the results of a survey that indicates margarine's positive contribution to a healthful diet.

In this era of increasing specialization, there are firms that do only financial PR and many larger firms that have financial departments. One firm, Ruder Finn, has a large division devoted to health care communications. Its clients range from major pharmaceutical and health care companies to small biotechnology firms and hospitals.

PR counsel firms in New York attract some of the best and brightest university graduates. Many, such as Ruder Finn, conduct competitive training programs that have enabled them to recruit M.B.A.s, Ph.D.s, and people with degrees in journalism, philosophy, science, and other disciplines. Tough competition, but it's worth it when you get there.

THE MANY NAMES OF PR PEOPLE

In the Introduction I referred to Richie Roberts as a "press agent." Most PR professionals consider this a pejorative term. Yet in the theater and allied entertainment fields, it is still widely used. A "publicist," a term that in most cases is synonymous with that of "press agent," is a person who spends most of the time trying to get stories written or broadcast about his or her clients. On Broadway, there is even a press agents' union, and so a running Broadway show is required to have a press agent who is paid a fixed amount—say, $1,500 to $2,000 a week—to publicize that particular production.

A less flattering term is "flack." The name is said to derive from Gene Flack, a one-time movie publicity agent. Columnists still use it as a disparaging term for press agents.

The title "spokesperson" is used frequently by the media to designate an organization's key PR representative. *PR News* describes the title as "disparaging, incorrect, and irritating," implying that the spokesperson is merely a mouthpiece, having nothing to do with formulating or implementing programs and policies. Nevertheless, the terms "spokesman" and "spokesperson" are widely used, particularly in government, governmental agencies, and large corporations.

At a corporation, the term "Director of Public Relations" is a popular designation for that individual who directs the company's entire PR effort. This title is "Director of Corporate Communications" in some organizations. A "Media Relations Director" is the individual whose efforts are concentrated on placing stories and releases in the print and broadcast media.

In recent years, the terms "spin" and "spin doctors" have become popular in political circles. Spin doctors are those engaged in manipulating public perceptions. "Spin" has a slightly negative connotation from a PR standpoint because it implies "image fixing." In a later chapter we'll discuss the successful career of John Scanlon, a prominent New York practitioner who has been labeled a spin doctor.

Other job titles used in PR are "Public Affairs Manager," "Communications Specialist," "Public Information Officer," "Press Secretary," "Information Representative," "Director of Community Relations," "Issues Communications Director," and "Consumer Affairs Director." There are differences in these job functions. A public affairs manager deals primarily with legislative and regulatory activity. A press secretary works for a public official and acts as that individual's link to the media. A consumer affairs director is concerned with a corporation's relationship with environmental and public-policy groups. These are terms used primarily by corporations and other organizations. At PR counsel firms, the title "Account Executive" seems to prevail. We discuss specific job functions in a later chapter.

HOW PR PROFESSIONALS ARE ACCREDITED

The Public Relations Society of America (PRSA; see Chapter 21 for its range of activities) is an accrediting organization for the PR profession. PR professionals with a minimum of five years' experience in the field qualify for PRSA accreditation by successfully completing a written and oral examination that tests their knowledge and competence in the practice of PR. They are then able to use the title APR (Accredited in Public Relations) after their names. Its importance is akin to that of a CPA certification in accounting.

PR: A TWO-WAY STREET

PR professionals spend a great deal of their time on placements—that is, arranging for their company's or client's releases and other information to appear in the media. However, as important as placements are for them, the journalists on the other side of the fence need a constant flow of news and feature material to satisfy the voracious appetites of print and broadcast media. This is especially the case in newspapers, where, studies have shown, half the content of the average newspaper comes from PR sources.

The highly respected *Washington Journalism Review* (*WJR*), with an audience of working journalists, publishes its *Directory of Selected News Sources* once a year. Here, hundreds of corporations and other organizations list their names and addresses, PR officers, and the kinds of information they have available. This listing facilitates the use of this material by the press.

In the section on agriculture, for example, six organizations, including the U.S. Department of Agriculture, are listed. No fewer than fourteen environmental groups are in the listing. A journalist choosing to do a feature piece on forest conservation has immediate access to the American Forestry Association, the Defenders of Wildlife, and The Wilderness Society.

In the same issue of *WJR* is a full-page ad from the New York Stock Exchange. Six press officers are listed with their phone numbers and specializations. The ad informs journalists that if they need information about stocks and bonds or the New York Stock Exchange itself, they should contact these press officers. This kind of ad may also suggest an article for a feature journalist.

In the following chapters we will analyze specifically the components of PR and how they work for different kinds of corporations and organizations.

PART II

Public Relations in Action

CHAPTER 3

The Components of PR

There are fourteen basic components of PR. We will briefly describe each of them and then discuss how they are managed within a PR counsel firm, a multinational corporation, governmental agencies, and various other organizations. Often these components overlap so that there is only a fine line of difference between, say, "strategic corporate PR" and "crisis communications."

Not every corporation or charitable organization will use all these components. The American Medical Association has little need for financial PR, but IBM's structure includes a large department involved in this activity. We offer an overview of these components here but will discuss them in greater detail later in the book.

Also keep in mind that a PR counsel firm operates outside a corporation's or organization's own PR department, performing certain duties supplemental to the in-house department.

MEDIA RELATIONS

Media relations may be the dominant function of PR. It concerns itself with packaging of press releases and "selling" them to the various media. Media relations people not only originate press information but also handle requests from the press about a company or organization's products and services.

Fred Clay, director of PR at Norton Simon, Inc., summed up the importance of media relations to a corporation: "The media is our consumer, our customer, if you will, and our product or service is news."

PUBLICATIONS, EMPLOYEE COMMUNICATIONS, AND EMPLOYEE RELATIONS

The preparation of quarterly and annual reports falls into the domain of this component of PR. The annual report is an extremely important "selling piece" for the corporation, with wide distribution to stockholders, brokers, security analysts, institutional investors, and those individuals considering investing in the company. Annual reports are issued by organizations as well as corporations. Employee communications people also prepare employee publications and newsletters.

SPEECHWRITING

Many large corporations have a "Chief Executive Speechwriter" whose main responsibility is writing speeches for CEOs. Speechwriters also write for other top executives. This component of PR is also carried out at organizations and government agencies. An adjunct of speechwriting is ghostwriting bylined articles for top executives for the trade and consumer press.

ISSUES COMMUNICATIONS

Issues communications and issues management fall under the purview of public affairs departments, primarily in corporations but in other organizations as well. Issues management deals with matters affecting the corporation in the present and potentially affecting it in the future. An organization might support a particular candidate in a political race, or run ads in newspapers and magazines regarding its position on social, environmental, and technical issues. Kentucky Fried Chicken, for instance, conducted a national campaign for Drug Abuse Resistance Education (DARE), which brings police officers into elementary schools to warn students about the dangers of drug use.

PUBLIC AFFAIRS AND LOBBYING

Public affairs PR helps the organization to understand, influence, communicate with, and adapt to its various publics: local and federal governments, governmental agencies, shareholders, and special-interest groups.

Lobbying involves interaction between an organization's representatives and governmental officials. Often it takes the form of influencing legislation or, in some cases, introducing new legislation affecting the organization's interest.

CORPORATE CONTRIBUTIONS AND PUBLIC SERVICE

In most organizations these two PR components fall within the organizational structure of the public affairs department. Most large corporations have policies concerning contributions. A contribution to public television to produce a particular series is an example of such corporate giving. Other examples might be the sponsorship of college scholarships or graduate fellowships, or of matching grants for cultural programs.

Public service enables a corporation to become directly involved in the local and national community. These programs may be in the areas of health and social action, arts and culture, and education.

In some companies the public-service effort is extensive and employs a large staff. These activities manifest a corporation's assumptions that public service is good business.

IMAGE BUILDING

Image building is a significant component of PR. Its implementation is the function of specialists within a corporation or organization and their PR counsel firms.

As an example of the use of image building by a large corporation, consider the following case. In October 1991 the Bristol-Myers Squibb Company received FDA approval for an AIDS treatment drug. Financial estimates placed the drug's revenues for the company at $100 million a year. Shortly after the approval, Bristol-Myers Squibb announced that it would provide this expensive drug free to those without the ability to pay for it. The company's PR staff distributed a report to the media on its policy regarding the drug. Clearly, this is positive image building targeted to a number of Bristol-Myers Squibb's publics—shareholders, the medical community, AIDS patients, governmental agencies, consumer groups, and the general public.

Other corporate image-building efforts have backfired. In 1990 Philip Morris sponsored a traveling exhibit of the original Bill of Rights. An advertising campaign featuring celebrities touting the Bill of Rights exhibit and tour drew fire from a number of consumer, environmental, and public-health organizations that considered the campaign "misleading and irresponsible" and charged that it "was designed to tie this document to its [Philip Morris's] so-called right to sell deadly products" (cigarettes).

COMMUNITY RELATIONS

"Community relations" refers to a corporation's or organization's activities in the local and national community. AT&T, for instance, assumes a broad-based role in the school reform process in Chicago's public schools. It is the job of the community relations staff to explore opportunities, secure the corporation's support, and then encourage the participation of employees. The community relations staff also publicizes these programs.

Many corporations include support for poverty and minority programs in their community relations agenda, as well as health care, cultural activities, and charitable contributions. The desired result: the molding of a positive corporate image.

STRATEGIC CORPORATE PR AND INTEGRATED COMMUNICATIONS

"Strategic corporate PR" and "integrated communications" seem to be the key buzz words in the PR field today. My old press agent friend Richie Roberts surely didn't know about strategic marketing and communications. His PR efforts were simple. You had a client whose name you got into the columns. Today the results of PR can be measured and evaluated, and its practitioners are held accountable for its results.

Strategic corporate PR is the identification of an objective—corporate staff downsizing, improved share price, greater productivity, more sales—and the implementation of an integrated program to achieve this objective.

In attaining these goals, says veteran senior PR executive Philip J. Webster, the corporation cannot succeed without "the assistance and alignment of the individuals and constituencies it relies on for support. In short, its publics or stakeholders, including employees, shareholders, the financial community, suppliers, plant communities, government, media, special interest groups, and the public at large."[4]

Integrated communications relates to the use of PR along with advertising, direct marketing, promotion, and other tools to shape public opinion and deliver audience actions. In practice, its effectiveness depends upon close cooperation between the corporation and its PR firm, and coordination through a single planning system of all the disparate elements.

FINANCIAL PR

The role of financial PR includes the task of communicating with the press, the shareholders of a corporation, or members of an organization regarding the organization's financial performance and objectives. This complex function involves preparing periodic and annual reports, arranging stockholders' meetings, writing press releases on earnings or the financial implications of new product development, and coordinating interviews between corporation or organization executives and security analysts.

Financial PR is a demanding activity calling for a broad range of skills on the part of its practitioners. It is also generally a well-paid job classification.

PERSONAL PR

During the divorce proceedings between Donald Trump and his wife, Ivana, each had a separate publicist. Every jab and counterpunch was trumpeted to the media for instant transmission to their gossip-hungry audience. If this seems to be overreacting personal PR, it is commonplace in Los Angeles, where one's publicist is as necessary as one's therapist.

In fact, in L.A. it's not just actors, rock stars, and athletes who have their own publicists; plastic surgeons, dentists who specialize in smile reconstruction, dog groomers, exercise physiologists, and even high-priced landscapers all retain PR specialists as well. It's as simple as this: Getting one's name in the newspapers or on TV is good business, justifying the monthly publicist's fee of $1,000 to $10,000.

One educator, Joan Konner, dean of Columbia University's Graduate School of Business, decries the "pollution" of the media with press releases that appear in the guise of journalism. Yet not all personal PR fits into the superficial mold. Having a publicist is a necessity in certain situations.

In 1987, an honor student at the U.S. Naval Academy, Joseph Steffan, was kicked out six weeks before graduation for revealing that he was gay. That's a no-no at Annapolis. Steffan fought the dismissal. He retained a publicist to get him on talk shows and in the print media to tell his story. He didn't gain his reinstatement, but he did draw much attention to the situation, and this could contribute to change in policy in the future.

Personal PR is a lucrative field employing thousands of publicists.

ADVOCACY PR

The public's vastly increased concern over environmental and public-health issues has spawned the organization of thousands of advocacy groups. Often these groups engage in bitter battles with industry and government over the resolution of key issues.

In a 1990 election in California, five ballot initiatives were offered to voters. They involved such sensitive areas as timber harvesting, alcohol taxes, marine resources, pesticide regulation, and the use of prison inmate labor. Each issue was contested by advocacy groups on one side and business and labor unions on the other.

This component of PR has developed discrete techniques in the implementation of its programs. It presents a particular challenge for advocacy groups, since they are almost always outspent by their opponents.

ENTERTAINMENT PR

The legendary P. T. Barnum of "There's a sucker born every minute" fame was a master of PR as far back as the mid–nineteenth century, when he established the first American circus. His showbiz heirs have carried on the tradition well.

In the theater, particularly on Broadway, each running show must have its own publicist. These people are not on the producer's or theater owner's staff but instead are independent and may work on more than one show at a time. During a show's run the publicist will feed items to the press and arrange interviews for its stars.

Record companies have their own PR staffs, but their artists have personal publicists to promote their tours and concerts.

In TV, the major networks publicize their shows, but often a show's production company will supplement this activity.

Although many movie actors have their own publicists, the studios maintain large PR staffs under the umbrella of Ad/Pub departments, combining the functions of advertising and publicity. Ad/Pub people publicize each movie on the studio's release list. This process begins as early as the signing of cast and director and continues until the movie completes its run, or even until it airs on cable television, comes out as a video, or spawns a sequel. Ad/Pub people also conduct and evaluate test screenings where they gauge audience reaction. They also organize and promote premieres.

Each movie has its own unit publicist who works with the studio's people arranging trade publicity and magazine, newspaper, and TV stories that will break on the movie's release. For a major movie the studio or distributor will generally arrange press breakfasts in New York and Los Angeles the week before the picture's release. At these meetings the press is able to interview the director of the movie, the screenwriters, and the stars. The media are also given press kits, which supply background information and thus aid in the preparation of feature stories and reviews.

For a movie featuring major stars, the PR team arranges interviews on major TV talk shows. If handled effectively, this form of PR can be more productive than advertising—and a lot cheaper.

Entertainment PR may seem to be a glamorous field, and in some respects it is. However, it is very stressful and highly competitive.

CORPORATE ADVERTISING

Although advertising people are involved in corporate advertising, it is also a component of public relations. Bill Cantor, in his book *Experts in Action: Inside Public Relations,* defines the purpose of corporate advertising: "To call attention to the company or to separate it from its competitors in the eyes of the financial community, shareholders, customers, employees and other important audiences."[5]

Corporate advertising does not sell a particular product. Instead, it offers the company's position on issues or situations. It is sometimes called institutional advertising.

An ad for Sandoz Pharmaceuticals Corporation in the *Los Angeles Times* illustrated one use of corporate advertising. Under a heading of "POLITICS VS. PATIENT SAFETY" the ad, in an all-type editorial style, sought to put forth its point of view on the issues on Sandoz's breakthrough drug Clozaril, used in treatment of schizophrenia.

Although the drug often works where standard therapies fail, there have been blood disorder side effect deaths in a small percentage of patients. Sandoz instituted a patient management system that controls the drug treatment therapy. However, lawsuits have been filed in more than twenty states and by lawyers for patients alleged to have been injured or killed by the drug's side effects.

From a PR standpoint, Sandoz would have difficulty placing stories in the press that are as persuasive as this ad. Also, by placing the ad in the financial section, Sandoz reaches the investment community with its message.

Other examples of corporate advertising might be an ad for Georgia-Pacific, a paper manufacturing company, defending its logging practices in the Pacific northwest; or an ad for Sears, Roebuck and Company discussing its minority hiring practices; or one for Chrysler Corporation recommending a "Buy America" campaign for consumers.

The preparation of corporate advertising is a province of a corporation's or organization's PR department, its outside PR counsel firm, and its advertising agency.

CRISIS COMMUNICATIONS

Bhopal, Love Canal, Three Mile Island, Lockerbie, *Exxon Valdez*—a litany of disasters no less infamous in the eyes of the public than the battle sites of war. In Bhopal, India, an explosion at a Union Carbide chemical plant caused the death of thousands. For years afterward Union Carbide's image was marred.

The *Exxon Valdez* oil spill in Alaska cost the company hundreds of millions of dollars and aroused the concerns of environmentalists worldwide. Management's poor handling of the crisis was widely criticized by the media.

Incidents such as those alluded to here—air crashes, product recalls, strikes, major accidents, attacks by environmental or advocacy groups, bankruptcies, and other emergencies that threaten the existence of a corporation or institution—require crisis communications and crisis management. The area of crisis communications provides the high drama of PR.

In a crisis the corporation or organization and its PR firm enlist the services of many people—writers to issue releases to the media, on-site personnel to work with local and national press, speechwriters for the organization's spokespersons, and contact people to make arrangements for meetings between the organization's executives and local officials.

In later chapters we devote considerable coverage to this vital component of PR. We discuss the proactive approach to crisis communications and management and examine an organization's crisis planning, its execution, and its evaluation of the results.

CHAPTER 4

The PR Counsel Firm: Structure and Function

Many corporations have large advertising departments but nonetheless employ ad agencies to prepare and place their advertising. Similarly, a corporation or other organization will have its own PR department but will employ an *outside* PR counsel firm for the special expertise it brings to the organization, corporation, or individual client.

We refer to this type of organization as the PR counsel, PR firm, or independent PR organization. It functions very much like an advertising agency. In fact, many PR firms are owned by advertising agencies.

The outside PR firm advises and counsels top management of an organization on many specialized areas of PR. It may also plan and stage events, functions, and even stunts. It often plans a whole year's program for its corporate and association clients. In a takeover or merger and acquisition, a PR counsel firm may orchestrate the entire strategic communications plan.

In media relations, the PR firm may handle inquiries from the press. It will also do its best to place news and feature stories in the media. These are commonly referred to as "placements." As with my old friend Richie Roberts, who did PR for restaurants, if you don't get enough placements, or "ink" as they refer to it, you lose the account. At times, however, it is the PR firm's job to keep a client's name *out* of the press.

WHAT PR FIRMS DO

In contrast to the practice of advertising, where job titles at an agency and those at an advertiser are totally different, in PR the jobs at an organization and at a counsel firm are similar. Also, job titles are not sharply defined and may vary from organization to organization. Starting at the entry level, here are the classifications.

Trainee or Assistant Account Executive

A trainee is assigned to one or more account groups. These include Consumer Marketing, Investor Relations, Financial Services, Health Care, Food/Lifestyle, Public Affairs, Arts, Visual Technology, and Hi-Tech. For these groups, the trainee or assistant performs a variety of functions.

He or she may be asked to develop and verify media lists—that is, to compile lists of print and broadcast media and the names of the individuals at these media sources to whom releases are to be directed. Although the PR firm maintains such lists, they must be constantly updated because of high turnover.

The trainee/assistant is often given an opportunity to write press releases and send "pitch" letters—missives suggesting a proposed interview or story—accompanying a press release to a reporter, editor, or broadcast news person. He or she will be indoctrinated early on in the techniques of the phone pitch—the call pitching to an editor a story.

Special events—awards ceremonies, groundbreakings, the introduction of a new product line, anniversaries—are the life blood of public relations. The trainee helps in their planning and, of course, attends them to work on details. He or she participates in creative and planning sessions for the firm's accounts and accompanies the account group when it visits the client.

At one large PR firm, Ruder Finn, trainees are hired for a four-month period at $1,250 per month. They function as assistant account executives and attend classes during their work schedule. The company ultimately hires about half of the graduates of its training program. Successful graduates become assistant account executives at a much higher salary.

Writing ability is a prime requisite for entry-level jobs at PR firms. At Ruder Finn, applicants are given an informational letter from the president of American Can Company on the introduction of a new public-service program and asked to write a short press release based on this information.

In another test, Ruder Finn gives applicants a short press release on the introduction of a new china dinnerware line by one of its clients. The applicant must write a one-page pitch letter to the *New York Times, Parent's Magazine,* and *Business Week.*

Account Executive

An account executive performs some of the functions of the assistant account executive but is more involved in the creative and planning aspects of PR. In this respect, he or she will maintain a great deal of client contact. In a large firm one rises to this job assignment in two or three years. The median salary nationwide is about $29,000. In the east it is about $34,250.

Senior Account Executive/Account Supervisor

The title varies according to the size of the PR firm, but the work of a senior account executive or account supervisor entails the supervision of a very large account or a number of smaller ones. The median salary nationwide is about $51,000; in the east, about $56,000.

Senior Manager/Senior Counselor

The position of a senior manager or senior counselor is a top managerial one at a PR firm. It involves the supervision of a number of people and a group of accounts. Often this individual "controls" an account. That is, he or she is responsible for bringing that account into the firm. The median salary nationwide is about $65,000. In the east it is about $74,000.

HOW MUCH DO THEY MAKE?

The good people at PRSA's *PR Journal* publish an annual salary survey. The August 1992 issue reported results of a study conducted by David Y. Jacobson and Nicholas J. Tortorello of Research & Forecasts, a division of Ruder Finn.

> • The median salary for all PR practitioners, inside corporations and other organizations, as well as at independent PR counsel firms, is about $47,000.
> • The highest median salary is likely to be found in corporate jobs; the lowest, in governmental, health care, and nonprofit organizations. Salaries at PR counsel firms fall in between.
> • The east is the best-paying region, followed by the west, the midwest, and the south.
> • As in most fields, women still earn less than men. How much less? The median salary for men with less than five years' experience is 15 percent higher than the median for women at the same level.
> • In answer to the question "Is it harder for women than men to reach the top in PR?", 35 percent of the men and 66 percent of the women responded affirmatively.

Regional considerations and length of experience affect the results. Less than half the respondents in public relations firms (41 percent) and corporations (47 percent) received bonuses. The median bonus for men was about $5,700 and about $2,100 for women.

Although public relations is a relatively low-paying field, it is more stable than advertising, where salaries are higher. Also to be considered are bonuses and perks. Of all respondents to this survey, 23 percent in PR firms received company cars or paid parking or both, and 19 percent of those working for corporations participated in stock-purchase plans. See Tables 1 and 2.

TABLE 1   SALARIES: MEN AND WOMEN, BY AGE (NOT INCLUDING BONUSES)

	MEDIAN SALARY
All respondents	$46,556
Under 35 years old	
Men	38,022
Women	32,109
35 years and older	
Men	62,911
Women	47,635

TABLE 2   SALARY BY TITLE, TYPE OF ORGANIZATION AND GENDER

JOB TITLE	MEDIAN SALARY
Account Executives	
Public relations firm	$28,132
Corporation	35,724
Government/health care/nonprofit	30,429
Median for Men	36,561
Median for Women	29,566
Supervisors	
Public relations firm	$49,713
Corporation	58,040
Government/health care/nonprofit	46,380
Median for Men	60,290
Median for Women	44,688
Senior Management	
Public relations firm	$63,814
Corporation	77,503
Government/health care/nonprofit	63,717
Median for Men	75,655
Median for Women	50,970

What type of organization you work in makes a difference in what you will earn. Table 3 shows some median salaries for various kinds of organizations.

TABLE 3

	MEDIAN SALARY
Industrial/manufacturing	$61,496
Public relations counseling firm	50,216
Scientific/technical	51,791
Association/foundation	42,841
Government	43,420
Health care	42,424
Religious/charitable	34,150

The area of PR you work in also influences how much you'll make. Table 4 shows some median salaries for various phases of PR.

TABLE 4

	MEDIAN SALARY
Investor relations	$65,173
Issues management	54,749
Generalist	49,303
Corporate communications	50,770
Media relations	47,301
Community relations	45,846
Publicity	45,434

CHAPTER 5

A Look at Five of the Largest PR Firms

There are thousands of public relations counsel firms, and, as we have seen, they perform a variety of services for a variety of clients. Many PR firms are small one- and two-person operations. In New York, the headquarters of PR, only the top thirteen firms employ one hundred or more people. The large firms make PR history every day. They're sought out by governments, corporations, associations, trade commissions, and even individuals. If you're talented enough, you may get to work for one of them. Let's take a close look at five of the largest.

BURSON-MARSTELLER

In New York, Burson-Marsteller employs about 550 people and handles 361 clients. That's 1.537 people per client. Account executives work in teams on more than one account at a time. In a crisis situation, the whole team may work for only one client.

Burson-Marsteller was founded in 1953. It is now owned by advertising giant Young & Rubicam. It maintains 58 offices in 26 countries throughout the world, employs about 2,500 people, and has worldwide billings of over $160 million annually. For PR counsel firms that's an enormous figure. In Asian and European markets Burson-Marsteller is number one in PR and public affairs in terms of size and billings.

The services Burson-Marsteller provides include corporate communications, consumer marketing, investor relations, crisis communications, research, issues analysis, and event marketing.

On any given day Burson-Marsteller may be found helping clients list their stocks on the Zurich exchange, publicizing the introduction of a new line of jeans in Chicago, conducting a medical symposium in Tokyo or the south of France, or preparing client representatives to address issues in London or Hong Kong. Sound exciting? It is.

Although its parent company, Y&R, numbers among its clients dozens of multinational corporations, this fact alone does not guarantee Burson-Marsteller the PR business of these companies. It has to sell itself to each client. Conversely, Burson-Marsteller serves Coca-Cola, IBM, and General Electric. Y&R doesn't.

HILL AND KNOWLTON

The WPP Group, a global communications octopus with many tentacles in PR, owns Carl Byoir Associates, Ogilvy Adams & Rinehart Group, and Hill and Knowlton.

Size is no barometer of quality in PR, and although Hill and Knowlton is big, that's not what has established it as the world's premier PR/public affairs firm. Hill and Knowlton justifiably boasts that it is the "counsel of choice" for more than one-quarter of the world's largest corporations and one-third of the *Fortune 500*.

In one recent forty-eight-hour period, Hill and Knowlton helped nine CEOs and managing directors establish business dialogues with officials of the U.S., Japanese, Chinese, and Australian governments and two different committees of the European Parliament. At the same time it worked with marketing professionals in five countries on the introduction or revival of seven products, including computer software, a breakthrough health care treatment, a packaged food innovation, and a telecommunications system.

In the same two days its staff introduced a leading U.S. financial institution to top professionals in Great Britain and Germany, prepared the Wall Street presentations of two Asian and three European corporations, and counseled four other companies involved in takeover battles on three continents.

The results: During those forty-eight hours the front pages of the *Wall Street Journal,* the *Financial Times* of London, and the *International Herald-Tribune* and the news broadcasts of independent and state-owned TV networks in seven countries carried stories on nine Hill and Knowlton clients. Its actions and innovations affected business around the world.

Hill and Knowlton employs almost 2,000 people in 63 offices in 25 countries. Its client list includes American Airlines, IBM, Kodak, Mazda, Nintendo, Pepsi Cola, Procter & Gamble, SmithKline, Beecham, and Xerox.

OGILVY ADAMS & RINEHART GROUP

Advertising's grand old man David Ogilvy does not look with favor on interloping neophytes. When WPP Group's Martin Sorrell took over Ogilvy & Mather, Ogilvy is reported to have said, "I have this old-fashioned idea that people who run agencies should be ad people, not accountants." In a few years, however, Ogilvy and Sorrell became fast friends. Today Sorrell's company owns three of the most important PR firms in the world.

Ogilvy Adams & Rinehart Group comprises 55 offices in 34 countries and employs about 700 people. It is the third largest PR firm worldwide. The Group performs many of the same functions as its sister agency Hill and Knowlton, with some additions. Ogilvy Adams & Rinehart Group initiates and executes programs covering radio and TV training for CEOs, community and local government relations, educational and youth programs, internal and external communications audits, and attitudinal, motivational, and market research.

With hundreds of accounts, how, we may ask, does a company such as Ogilvy Adams & Rinehart Group service individual clients? Every client has an Ogilvy PR Account Group Director who interfaces with the CEO or other top executive at the client company or organization. In addition, Ogilvy PR has an internal review board to monitor its progress on each account.

Ten Ogilvy PR clients represent 20 percent of its income. They include the American companies American Express, Bristol-Myers, the Ford Foundation, and Mattel, as well as the multinationals Philips, Shell, and Unilever. Twenty-five of its clients are represented in five or more countries.

RUDER FINN

Founded in 1948, Ruder Finn is today an organization of almost 300 people with fee income of $37 million annually. It also owns a medical marketing and research subsidiary. Ruder Finn headquarters are in New York and Paris, and it has wholly-owned offices in Boston, Chicago, London, Los Angeles, Manchester, Raleigh, Stockholm, Tokyo, and Washington, D.C., as well as a worldwide affiliate network.

The parent company services clients in many industries and organizations, but one specialization has led to the establishment in the 1970s of Ruder Finn Health Care Communications to serve pharmaceutical and health care companies, biotechnology firms, hospitals, and professional associations.

Another area of Ruder Finn's specialization is public affairs. In this area Ruder Finn employs former senior congressional and presidential staff members, professional journalists, and legislative analysts. These specialists integrate PR strategies with lobbying objectives to increase the effectiveness of their clients' governmental relations programs. This function may include such sophisticated techniques as the research, writing, and printing of congressional testimony and the preparation of press releases and lobbying support materials.

Incidentally, Ruder Finn conducts the largest and most competitive executive training programs in the industry. (More about this in a later chapter.)

EDELMAN PUBLIC RELATIONS WORLDWIDE

With 23 offices and 50 affiliates, Edelman Public Relations Worldwide is the sixth largest PR firm in the world. This 50-year-old agency employs about 500 people and is active in every facet of PR. Edelman engages in diverse activities for many multinational companies.

For Weight Watchers/Heinz, Edelman runs a health, nutrition, and fitness program in the United States, Great Britain, and France. One specific program is a three-day workshop entitled "Expert Workshop on Human Eating Behavior." Heinz continues to spend advertising dollars in these markets, but its sponsorship of workshops positions the Weight Watchers brand as acting in the public interest, not just as an advertiser.

When British Airways sought to revive a sagging business after the Persian Gulf crisis in 1991, Edelman ran a sweepstakes promotion in dozens of countries; 5.7 million people participated.

Special events afford excellent publicity opportunities, and the possibilities are limited only by the ingenuity of the sponsors. Edelman mobilized the entire town of Corbin, Kentucky, where Colonel Sanders opened his first Kentucky Fried Chicken restaurant, to celebrate the centennial of his birth.

For Edelman's client Advil, the pitcher Nolan Ryan was named spokesperson for its SportSense program. In a similar promotion for DuPont, Edelman generated name recognition and good will by publicizing the story of Bill Demby, a Vietnam veteran now freed from his wheelchair because of an innovative prosthesis built with DuPont's Delrin product.

Few of these promotions are totally original, but when they are orchestrated and implemented effectively by a PR firm such as Edelman Worldwide, they provide important adjuncts to a company's advertising and marketing program.

A SHORT TALK WITH
HOWARD J. RUBENSTEIN

I first met Howard Rubenstein more than twenty years ago. He was handling PR for the fledgling Weight Watchers organization, and I was publishing its magazine. Under his nurturing Weight Watchers grew into a strong national organization that was later purchased by H. J. Heinz.

Since then Rubenstein has become an influential force in New York PR and political affairs. His firm is the eighth largest in New York, with a client list of the mighty and the celebrated. I asked him a few questions about his practice and his profession.

According to a recent listing, your firm handles 350-plus clients with a staff of about 140. Most other large firms have a higher ratio of employees to clients. How do you do it?

We are results-oriented and bottom-line-conscious. Our efforts are directed toward meeting the client's business goals. While we understand and highly value the importance of learning and listening, we do not waste time on unnecessary frills and meetings for the sake of meeting. Our objective is not to describe what we are going to do, but to do it—to break major stories in key media.

We have a highly professional staff capable of honing a story, packaging it intelligently, and presenting it persuasively to the appropriate reporters.

All professional staff members have account responsibilities. No one simply manages others. We also utilize a team approach where appropriate for major, complex assignments. Each contributes what he or she does best in a dynamic, creative, and efficient mix.

Your firm handles such high-voltage personalities as Donald Trump and Rupert Murdoch. Is their PR managed on an issue-by-issue basis, or is it based on a strategic plan? Do their organizations have their own PR departments, and, if so, how do you interact with them?

It is crucial in all accounts—and particularly so with so-called "high voltage" clients—to understand their operations and their objectives. Since these clients are in the public eye, they are inevitably both newsmakers and targets. There must be an overall strategy to ensure that you are moving in the right direction. But every issue must also be evaluated on a day-by-day basis, with continuing input from the client or his designated representative, to meet the internal logic of each situation, to exploit its full potential (or minimize its damage). A number of our clients do have their own PR departments, and we work well with them. Basically, we extend their reach.

The important factor is to speak with one voice, theirs or ours, which reflects the best judgments made after appropriate consultation and review.

In a magazine article, one PR professional said of you, "He won't call a press conference unless there's news; [he] has the best-attended press conferences in New York." How do you go about conducting a conference? Is it done with just a press release, or is there telephone follow-up to the media?

There are four basic rules regarding press conferences:

• *Make sure you are making news*—either because of what you're saying or who's saying it, or both;

• *Have a powerful visual.* Rarely rely on just talking heads, even if they're heads of state;

• *Hold the press conference in an accessible location at a realistic time.* Make certain the room fits the event, for there is little worse than a low turnout in a vast space; be flexible so that you can add (or remove) seats as needed;

• *Don't schedule your press conference for a time (or a day) when you know a major competing story will be breaking.*

Inform the press about the conference by releasing a "tip sheet," a catchy announcement—sent out a few days prior to the event—which is designed to entice but omits the hard news. Follow up with phone calls and faxes the day before and morning of the press conference. After the press conference make sure you and your client are available to respond to further queries, as well as to arrange for "beeper" interviews. (The beeper allows the press to reach the PR person or interviewee any time following the press conference.) Send the press kit to all appropriate media not present. It's also usually a good idea to have your own photographer there so you can service the wires [wire services], if they are interested, and the trades.

How do you work with the trash tabloids that prey on celebrities like Donald Trump?

We serve as heat shields or buffers, as appropriate, and politely decline any interviews [the clients] may not wish to do. Our clients, in consultation with us, set the ground rules so that we can make informed judgments about how best to serve their interests. Some questions or allegations don't deserve the dignity of a response. For many, "no comment" will do. For others, it may be important to squelch a rumor or present a position.

As a fast-growing organization, you obviously are increasing staff. Where do you look for new people?

I believe we have a great staff of Tiffany-quality professionals. Many have been with me for many, many years. Among the qualities I value most are the ability to listen well, to understand a client's needs rather than talk a loud, uninformed blue streak; solid business and political judgment; fast and facile writing; adherence to the highest ethical standards, both personal and professional; commitment and a desire to work hard, which is crucial in a service business like ours; and a love of the profession. My top people—and those I continue to seek out—come from government, private-sector companies, other agencies, and the media.

CHAPTER 6

How PR Works
at a Giant Multinational
Corporation

IBM, the world's largest computer company, employs more people than live in Minneapolis. It is the nation's fourth largest industrial company, with annual revenues exceeding $60 billion. In the second half of the 1980s it had slipped into a dangerous slump. Its stock price had gone from as high as $173 a share in 1987 to a low of $93 in December 1989. Clearly, Wall Street and investors alike were down on the company. What to do?

In late December 1990 IBM called a press conference. The financial press and stock analysts were invited. IBM's media relations people arranged the meeting and handled the invitations. Press kits with current sales and financial data were given to all in attendance.

On Monday, December 31, the *Los Angeles Times* ran a six-column story on page 4 of the financial section with a picture of an IBM executive in front of a PS/1 home computer and the headline "IBM Is on Rebound with Streamlined Operations, New Product Lines."[6] The story was bylined "From Associated Press."

The article in the *Times* revealed a refreshing openness on the part of IBM's executives. They sounded like Mikhail Gorbachev apologizing for the excesses of previous Soviet governments. IBM took the heat for its outdated and overpriced products and its bloated payroll and cost structure.

The "new" IBM, they claimed, is reducing its payroll, shipping all it can build of a new mainframe line, and buying minority stakes in dozens of small software houses. Summing it all up, Frank A. Metz Jr., IBM's chief financial officer, said, "We also did some real introspection and concluded that part of the problem was ours. . . . [IBM] must reemphasize our commitment to our customer. . . . We concluded that, although our products were good, it was taking us too long to get our products to the marketplace, and too often they weren't as responsive as they need to be to our customer requirements."

Press conferences and candor may not counteract the vagaries of the marketplace—by the end of 1992 IBM still had not come out of the woods, and its stock had fallen to its lowest level in eleven years. Yet a piece like the *Times* article does have a positive impact. It reassures many of IBM's publics—individual investors, financial institutions, stock analysts, stockholders, dealers, and employees—as to the direction of the company. It is an example of PR at its most effective.

THE MEDIA RELATIONS DEPARTMENTS

With a company as large as IBM, the PR function is divided into different divisions. IBM has two main divisions, Corporate Media Relations, and Marketing and Services Media Relations. IBM Corporate Media Relations is responsible for issues and financial matters that have an impact on IBM worldwide, while Marketing and Services is concerned with IBM's products and services in the United States.

At IBM Corporate Media Relations, assignments are split up into nine separate groups or departments, each headed by a corporate media relations specialist. Some of these groups are responsible for a dozen different issues. For the purpose of clarity, we designate each department with a group number.

IBM CORPORATE MEDIA RELATIONS

Group 1

Financial Issues

Security Analysts

Board of Directors Issues

Proxy Issues

Stockholders Meetings

Corporate Equity Agreements

Corporate Organization

Group 2

Technology Issues and Developments

Strategic Technology

Corporate Manufacturing and Development

Research Issues

IBM Fellows

Quality/Baldridge Award

Group 3

Worldwide Personnel Issues

full employment, compensation and benefits,

equal opportunity, industrial relations,

employee litigation, air travel advisories/IBM aircraft

Employee Health and Safety

VDTs/ergonomics, AIDS, drug/liquor policy

Education Issues

internal IBM education, external education programs

Group 4

World Trade Issues

technology transfer, international trade,

IBM as transnational, European Community, exports,

balance of trade, international alliances

Environmental Issues

Group 5

Intellectual Property Issues (patents, copyrights, trademarks)

Litigation (except employee)

Internal Information Systems
IBM Design Program
Corporate Sponsorship

Group 6
Products
    corporate marketing, strategic directions,
    supply/demand, positioning of products in relationship to
    each other, usability, customers
Business Relationships
    purchasing, consultants, business partners
Industry Relations
    data security/privacy, viruses, standards

Group 7
Federal/State Procurement
IBM Governmental Activity
    congressional visits to IBM sites, IBM visits to congressional
    offices, IBM Washington office operations, Honoraria, PACs

Group 8
South Africa
Education
    legislation, business roundtable activities
Other Legislation
    technology, environment, personnel,
    health/safety/VDTs

Group 9
Tax Legislation
    local/state/federal tax initiatives
Export/Trade
Pension Legislation

The people employed in IBM's media relations department originate press information and handle constant requests from the press
about their specialties. They write and prepare printed material on
their subject areas. Often they are called on to write speeches for

executives on quick notice. In some departments, such as World Trade Issues, key staffers are political scientists, trained to deal with the sensitive subjects of international trade and relations.

The areas of World Trade Issues and Environment Issues involve seven sub-issues: technology transfer, international trade, IBM as a multinational corporation, European Community, exports, balance of trade, and international alliances.

Each sub-issues section is headed by a press officer responsible for a number of areas. There is always a backup person for each area should that individual be unavailable when reporters call. Each media relations officer must have consummate expertise in his or her area. A misquote on the telephone can have dire repercussions.

In the event of a crisis, let's say a one-day drop of six or seven points in IBM's stock due to sharply reduced earnings, all the department heads in Corporate Media Relations have been trained to deal with the media on this situation.

The media relations people in Federal/State Procurement and IBM Governmental Activity are based in Washington and include lobbyists familiar with the activities of legislative and executive bodies. They arrange congressional visits to IBM sites and IBM visits to congressional offices.

THE MARKETING AND SERVICES DIVISION

IBM's Marketing and Services Division has six separate sections:

Services and Marketing Media Relations
Software Products and Advanced Work Stations Media Relations
Desktop Systems Media Relations
Enterprise, Midrange and Communication Systems Media Relations
IBM U.S. Employee and Community Media Relations
IBM Research Communications Media Relations

The Marketing and Services director's scrutiny extends over each of these sections. Within a section, such as Services and Marketing, there are many subsections, each headed by a press officer. If IBM introduces a major new software line, for example, it is publicized by the Software Products Media Relations department of this division.

IBM AND THE COMMUNITY

Most annual reports devote a few pages to the philanthropic and public affairs activities of their companies. IBM is no exception. Its top management has directed the public relations staffers who prepare the annual report to convey the image that IBM is a company with a real corporate conscience, especially in its policies concerning the assistance and hiring of women, minorities, and the disabled. The annual report points out that IBM employs 26,000 Vietnam-era and disabled veterans, that minorities hold about 13 percent of their U.S. management positions and women hold over 20 percent, whereas in senior management positions minorities hold about 10 percent and women about 13 percent.

How do these policies affect IBM's publics? Do you buy an IBM P.C. instead of an Epson because you are impressed with IBM's hiring policies? Probably not. IBM derives only an intangible, though still important, benefit from this enlightened approach.

Whether it's an affirmative action program or its annual contributions of almost $140 million to social, cultural, and educational programs worldwide, for IBM it's all part of image building. This may manifest itself in someone's buying fifty shares of IBM stock, saving it for a lifetime, and leaving it to his children. Or it might be a talented black computer science graduate making the decision to go with IBM rather than other companies recruiting her.

IBM has plants and offices around the country but maintains its headquarters in New York. It hires entry-level people at the assistant account executive level.

*   *   *

Within a large corporation's or organization's staff there are a number of other specialists with a variety of functions and responsibilities. They include:

• *Director, Educational Activities:* coordinates organization's relationship with schools, colleges, and the academic community.

• *Coordinator, Speakers' Bureau:* arranges for organization's officers' speeches before trade and public groups.

• *Manager, Public Information Department:* manages organization's information flow to the press and the public.

• *Editor, House Organ and Special Publications:* supervises the preparation of in-house publications.

In addition to these individuals, organizations employ PR people as researchers, writers, news specialists, photographers, and audio/visual producers.

CHAPTER 7

How PR Works
at Other Organizations

We have defined the role of the PR counsel firm and how PR works at a multinational corporation. In this chapter we'll examine how PR is carried out at other organizations.

PR FOR A NONPROFIT HEALTH ORGANIZATION

The American Heart Association is the public's leading authority and advocate on cardiovascular health and science. It operates on an annual budget of more than $277 million. Its public support and revenues come from individual and corporate contributions, legacies and bequests, support from local fund-raising agencies, and governmental agencies. Its network of volunteers exceeds 3.5 million in more than 2,000 state, territorial, and local divisions across the country.

Where is this money spent? Research, public health education, professional education and training, and community services are the recipients of about $190 million, with the balance going for support services, an area that includes all the organization's operating expenses.

How does the American Heart Association implement its aggressive communications program? At the top level, headquartered in Dallas, a Vice President of Communications directs an extremely comprehensive communications program. This Office of Communications is responsible for two divisions. Corporate Communications includes Public Relations, Editorial/Media Productions, Design, and Client Services. Health and Science News includes Media Inquiries, News Conferences, Video News Releases, and News Releases for the print media.

The headquarters Office of Communications employs about forty people. Following are the responsibilities of each section.

• *Public Relations:* provides communications consultation to affiliates on volunteer and staff training and assistance with media issues.

• *Editorial/Media Productions:* develops and writes fund-raising, educational, and promotional materials; produces *American Heart News,* a quarterly publication, as well as newspaper columns, recipes, and features for the media; develops, produces, and maintains all audio/visual materials and programs for the AHA.

• *Design:* provides illustrations, photography, typesetting, and graphic design services.

• *Client Services:* coordinates and manages work flow of all print and audio/visual materials.

• *Health and Science News:* is responsible for all contacts with and programs directed to the news media, including the specialized science media. The department handles more than 4,000 media inquiries annually and produces news packets for scientific meetings, including the largest meeting of its kind in the world: the American Heart Association Scientific Sessions.

The AHA is an exciting place to practice a PR career. It employs editors, writers, speechwriters, art directors, media relations specialists, photographers, and audio/visual specialists. There are other organizations similar to it all over the country.

PR IN GOVERNMENT AND GOVERNMENTAL AGENCIES

In Chapter 11 we discuss the area of public affairs and lobbying. These are basically efforts dealing with government intervention on behalf of corporations and other organizations. On the government side are the people whose concern is promoting and publicizing the activity of their federal, state, and local agency, all of whom use and practice PR. Practically every official above the rank of police lieutenant has a press spokesperson who sends out press releases, conducts interviews, and writes speeches for appointed officials. In addition, in the U.S. Congress, each senator and representative has a press aide.

Consider the front page of the *Los Angeles Times* for October 18, 1991. Eight of the nine news stories emanated from the press offices of various governmental agencies. The list included the U.S. Senate Judiciary Committee, the California State Attorney General, NATO, the Senate Ethics Committee, the U.S. House of Representatives, the Labor Department, the Christopher Commission of the State of California, and the police chief's office of the city of Killeen, Texas.

PR jobs in the governmental sector are demanding and stressful. A press spokesperson does not merely issue press releases; he or she also handles press conferences.

Here's an example of PR at a state agency:

In 1989 the Connecticut Department of Transportation, a typical state agency, conducted a campaign to reduce congestion on the state highways, called "Ride Together, Connecticut—It's the Best Way to Work." A case study in *PR News* detailed the efforts undertaken by the agency to get people to use car pools. Radio, newspapers, highway signs and billboards, and brochures were used to sell the message— at a cost of $250,000. City buses helped promote the campaign. Employee publications statewide featured "Ride Together" articles. The result: 33,800 commuters joined a car pool, and others became more aware of the problem.

PR FOR AN EDUCATIONAL ASSOCIATION OR INSTITUTION

A national teachers' organization, a college or university, or a state or local school board has similar objectives: to provide a favorable image of the group or institution and to deal with issues involving it with its publics. These may be legislatures, parents, alumni, or foundations.

Colleges and universities use PR extensively. At most institutions there is a press office charged with a variety of functions. These may include fund raising, giving awards, making policy changes, publicizing appointments, and so forth. Because sports are a prominent activity at most colleges, there is usually a sports information office apart from the schools' primary press operation.

Here is an example of PR in action at a state educational association. Concerned with the problems of lower educational standards, a high dropout rate, and overcrowded classes, the State of Washington Education Association, primarily a teachers' group, embarked on a blitz campaign to increase public awareness of the situation. An outside PR counsel firm was engaged to supplement the efforts of the association's own PR staff.

The first step was to identify the publics—legislators, the business community, and the media—and then research the issue in depth. A press release was sent to 365 newspaper, radio, and TV outlets, along with a photograph of a typically crowded classroom. Accompanying the release was a can of sardines with a label reading, "Do our children deserve to be packed like this in school?" Ads in various media tied in to this theme.

Direct mail was used as a follow-up. More than one hundred speeches were delivered by the group's leaders. Media coverage of the entire effort was extensive. The result: a 9 percent increase in public awareness of the problem and a large additional appropriation from the legislature for the state's education program.

PR FOR A PROFESSIONAL OR TRADE ASSOCIATION

The American Institute of Architects is a national group representing the interests of 55,000 architects in the United States. Its PR arm provides information on architectural design and practice, housing and urban issues, and designing with environmentally safe products.

The National Association of Social Workers is a 130,000-member group that provides information on social work practices in the United States and abroad.

The Society of Professional Journalists is a national organization that disseminates comments on press matters, including referrals on libel and freedom-of-information issues.

These three groups pursue active PR programs. To understand the workings of PR in this field, let's focus on one such group, the American Medical Association (AMA). The AMA represents almost 300,000 medical practitioners in the United States. Its communication activities are varied, part of an overall strategic plan aimed at strengthening public and professional confidence in the organization and its members. Here's how the AMA implements this program.

1. The Public Information Department handles well over 1,000 telephone calls a month from the news media and the public seeking socioeconomic and clinical information.

2. AMA officers and executives visit dozens of cities yearly on media tours.

3. Relevant AMA policies on medical ethics, the cost of health care, AIDS treatment, and other subjects are discussed in the media.

4. Officers and trustees make speeches before civic and business groups.

5. The AMA conducts science conferences in co-sponsorship with universities.

6. A weekly packet of AMA news releases is distributed to almost 3,000 journalists.

7. American Medical TV is a regular two-hour program on the Discovery Channel aimed at physicians and other health care professionals, as well as health-oriented consumers.

8. The AMA publishes *JAMA*, the highly respected *Journal of the American Medical Association,* with a domestic weekly circulation of approximately 380,000. It is also published in nine Asian and European editions.

9. As a function of its formidable lobbying program, the AMA is continually in touch with Congress, executive departments, and other federal agencies regarding health care issues and the interests of its members.

Many more communication and PR activities are carried out by the AMA. For our purposes, just think of the kinds of jobs available in such an organization. Science writers, editors, speechwriters, and media relations people are just a few that come to mind.

AN INTERVIEW WITH A SENIOR PR EXECUTIVE AT THE AMERICAN MEDICAL ASSOCIATION

Daniel Maier is currently the Director of News and Information at the American Medical Association and has handled virtually every medical issue for the past five years. Recently he directed the AMA's efforts against Old Joe Camel and media activities surrounding the AMA's call for health system reform. He is also an award-winning screenwriter and a published speechwriter.

Prior to joining the AMA, Mr. Maier was the press aide and speechwriter for U.S. Senator Alan Dixon of Illinois. He continues to be active in Illinois politics, organizing the Chicago suburbs for presidential campaigns and working as an adviser to Illinois congressional candidates.

Mr. Maier, a graduate of the University of Notre Dame, resides in Mt. Prospect, Illinois.

AMA officers and directors visit dozens of cities yearly to speak to the media and to meet with state and local medical-society officers. Arranging these tours necessarily involves a great deal of planning and detail. How is this operation managed at your office?

Every year the American Medical Association embarks on an active media schedule to bring the issues of medicine to the media and public rather than the other way around. In the past, public opinion and media interest have ruled the issues and topics of medicine. The medical profession was relegated to reacting to topics of questionable importance or significance to the American public.

In 1990, the AMA decided to take a more active role to bring the public health topics deemed important by physicians to national attention. One of the most successful methods of garnering media attention has been an activity called "media tours." Media tours are best compared to political campaign stops. Public-information officers are joined by a member of the AMA's Board of Trustees on a one- or two-day visit to the 200 largest cities in the country. Coordinated with the state and local medical societies, these tours' primary focus is to speak with the editorial boards of the local newspapers. Our theory is: The editorial board controls the paper, the paper drives the news of the area, and all local media read the local newspapers. No agenda is set; rather, we enter the editorial board with a clean slate. Whatever the paper wishes to discuss, we will discuss. However, we also bring topics that we wish to raise, from health system reform to national AIDS policy.

All planning and execution for the thirty-eight annual tours are in the hands of the public-information officers. We hire creative and independent people who are comfortable and adaptable in almost any situation. The tours are set up two to three weeks in advance and include the editorial boards, local science and health reporters, local business magazines, local television and radio programs, a meeting with the state or county medical society, and even a visit to a medical school, large hospital, or chamber of commerce. Although these tours make for a long and tiring day, most physicians are very active persons, able to handle the rigors of such a "campaign" stop.

The tours accomplish three simple goals for the AMA. First, we are seen and heard all around the country, from Alaska to Florida. Our offices of News and Information and Science News quickly build mailing lists and media contacts from around the country, making the AMA a primary resource for news and health information. And last, we are able to conduct speakers' training and deal with the media in the field with our two dozen spokespeople. The "on the road/in the field" training is by far the best opportunity to impart media experience. Classroom training will never be as effective as the intensive "classroom" of our media tours.

Following every tour, a full report on the topics discussed, performance of the trustee, and local acceptance of our trip are reported back to management. In short, this technique is an excellent method of gathering information about trends and advance warning on possible problems that might rise to national prominence. We can also field test ideas, products, or sound bites to see if they will fly in "Peoria."

Who does the speechwriting, and do these writers perform other functions as well?

The AMA speaks to several hundred audiences a year from all fields and in all corners of the country. Three full-time speechwriters produce approximately 200 speeches each year for about 24 different physician speakers. Speechwriting for a medical organization is challenging, but not lacking for topics, anecdotes, and apt metaphors. In addition, the speechwriters help in the preparation of optional editorials for newspapers and letters to the editor, depending on the topic.

In addition to arranging the speaking tours, what are your other communications and public relations duties?

Our staff of 10 PR professionals takes an average of 1,400 calls from the media each month on every topic imaginable. As a result of our media tours, we are often a clearinghouse of information and a quick-reference guide for reporters.

Approximately 60 percent of our inquiries are on socioeconomic–medical topics. Staff will either fulfill the request for information personally, refer the reporter to AMA staff with the necessary expertise, or arrange an interview with one of our twenty-four official physician spokespersons. Unfortunately, most of the twenty-four are practicing physicians scattered across the country. The logistics can be troublesome. However, AMA physicians realize the power and importance of the media and are eager to present the physician side to any question.

Of course, the AMA is involved in many topics that require press conferences or media briefings, usually in a major media center such as New York or Washington. All of these events are planned and executed through public relations with little trouble. We do attempt to be meager with press conferences so that the media know that the quality of the announcement will be meaningful. If the story to be announced is of smaller newsworthiness, we often try other means of release, such as a breakfast backgrounder. This forum is less formal and signifies an exchange of information that may or may not be worthy of immediate news. However, the information might be important in other news stories or foretell future news events.

Does the AMA engage outside PR counsel firms in addition to the in-house staff? What do they do?

The American Medical Association does not engage outside PR counsel. We hire highly motivated and creative people who are able to combine all the necessary skills to make the AMA the largest news source of medical information outside the federal government. By and large, outside firms are not able to match inside expertise or appreciate the many facets and intricacies of medical information and topics. However, we do invite PR professionals from the 300 other medical societies to Chicago [AMA headquarters] to provide outside perspectives and local expertise to our PR department. This type of counsel can provide timely and pertinent information from a medical perspective. We can commiserate and exchange problem-solving ideas.

Counsel from other medical organizations is a relatively inexpensive method compared with outside PR firms and fosters better relationship between all the medical societies. Our motto toward outside PR firms is, "Why ask your bachelor brother how to raise your children?"

PR FOR AN ADVOCACY ORGANIZATION

PR in an advocacy group is best understood by some examples. The Humane Farming Association is an advocacy group seeking humane treatment for animals on large factory farms. It conducts an information program through advertising and direct-mail campaigns.

Defenders of Wildlife is a Washington-based conservation organization that seeks to achieve its objectives through lobbying and awareness programs.

Earth Day is a major annual environmental effort. The parent organization coordinates local, national, and international activities. Corporations such as Monsanto, Hewlett-Packard, Apple Corporation, and the Chemical Manufacturers Association participate in Earth Day celebrations.

For Earth Day 1990—the twentieth anniversary of the event—the staff coordinated a media marketing campaign on a budget of $3 million, and used direct mail for fund raising. Thousands of people across the country took part in educational sit-ins, rallies, tree plantings, and other local events. The program was a brilliant success, illustrating PR and marketing at its best.

PR FOR RELIGIOUS GROUPS AND CHARITABLE ORGANIZATIONS

Many of the PR operations we have just discussed apply to religious groups and charitable organizations. The Religious Communications Congress of PR Professionals, which serves all denominations, publishes the *Religious PR Handbook*. There are a number of sub-organizations and publications in this field. Many PR people involved with religious groups are trained in theology.

A charitable organization deals with dozens of publics, including volunteers, donors, staff, clients, members, the media, governmental agencies, legislators, community groups, related organizations, the headquarters office, affiliates and field offices, and foundations.

To get its message across, a charitable organization uses news and video releases, leaflets and brochures, newsletters, speeches, press conferences, meetings and conventions, opinion polls, exhibits and displays, legislative bulletins, and special events.

According to Sunshine Janda, senior vice president of United Way of America, charitable organizations need PR practitioners because of the "huge impact on these organizations of the new societal trends, and competition for limited resources and volunteers." She concludes that not-for-profit PR is big business with a lot at stake.[7]

PART III

A Closer Look at the Components of Public Relations

CHAPTER 8

Media Placement and Media Relations

Howard R. Mitchell III, Vice President Public Relations, Keller-Crescent Company in Evansville, Indiana, sums up the essence of media relations.[8] Media relations programs should sell the editorial community on the informational value of a company (or organization), its people, and its products. As in any marketing effort, successful media relations depends on building an authentic rapport with the target audience (reporters and editors) while giving them something they can genuinely use.

Mitchell goes on to list some of the typical tasks of a media relations program, which are to

- Develop corporate or product positioning strategies for specific media outlets
- Plan photo and editorial opportunities for use in the media and develop editorial ideas to fit a publication's or broadcast medium's special promotions
- Develop news and feature releases for print and electronic media

- Gain favorable product reviews
- Place articles: case histories, editorials, features, "how to" stories, first-person angles, and so on
- Position client as an expert source for broad news and feature coverage
- Execute media events, media tours, and promotions
- Collect and analyze media coverage.

THE PRESS RELEASE OR NEWS RELEASE

The press or news release is at the heart of media relations.

The *Wall Street Journal* receives about 6,000 press releases a week. Many of these are two or three pages long. The major news agency, United Press International, receives 500 to 600 mailings a day. How can the staffs of these media sources possibly find time to read all this material? Experienced media relations people are well aware of this competition for placement of stories and strive to avoid the wastebasket with a number of techniques. One is brevity. A 200-word news story has a far better chance of being read by the editor and reporters beyond the lead paragraph. Another is the quality of the writing. The overall appearance of the press release is also a consideration. The news release for the American Heart Association shown in Fig. 1 is printed in two colors and uses desktop typesetting and laser printing to achieve an attractive, readable result. The reporter doesn't expect the media relations person to write the article but can usually tell from the opening sentences whether the release has merit.

Figure 1 is a news release issued by the American Heart Association. It reports on new findings by a group of medical investigators relating to job strain, high blood pressure, and heart disease. The results of these findings appeared in an American Heart Association scientific journal.

Press releases such as this one receive wide coverage. The media are always interested in a new development in this area, especially when it emanates from an authoritative source like the American Heart Association. The release is sent to health, medical, and science editors in the print and broadcast media.

We should note a few things about this release. First, the two authors of the release are listed on the upper right of the first page, along with their phone numbers and the code name of the report. Editors receiving the release who wish to receive the entire report can then contact Howard Lewis or John Weeks at the American Heart Association. Reporters or editors who wish to interview the medical researchers who came up with these findings can get their phone numbers from the "media advisory" on the bottom of page 2 of the release.

For purposes of confidentiality, we have blocked out the actual phone number.

The Elements of a Good Press Release

A good press release such as the one for the AHA should read the way a good news or feature story reads. The lead paragraph here concerns a subject—bypass surgery—that is frequently covered by newspapers and magazines. The research findings deal with a subject that is of immediate interest; therefore, the story has an excellent chance for wide placement.

In terms of structure, the press or news release submitted to the media must read like a news reporter's submission to his or her editor. That is, the lead paragraph must contain the same six elements we learned in Journalism 101: who? what? how? when? where? why?

The release should be just long enough to cover the subject. Short paragraphs make for easy reading. If a wire service chooses to do a one-hundred-word synopsis, it should easily be done from the release.

The release should be written in nontechnical language unless it is meant for technical or scientific journals.

A tailor-made or exclusive press release should be just that, written to the needs and style of the reporter or editor who will use it. A press release must express a point of view that hasn't been widely expounded elsewhere. The recipient in the media must often make an instant decision on its value as news.

News
Release

**American Heart
Association**

National Center
7320 Greenville Avenue
Dallas, Texas 75231

For Release:

AMs Thursday, July 9, 1992
(Broadcast: 5 p.m. EDT July 8)

NR 92-3998 (Circ/Peduzzi/Takaro)**
For more information contact:
Howard L. Lewis (214) 706-1340
John Weeks (214) 706-1330

News from AHA journals:

**BENEFITS OF BYPASS SURGERY FADE
AFTER A DECADE, STUDY SUGGESTS**

DALLAS, July 9 -- Beneficial effects of heart bypass operations done in
the early 1970s began to diminish after about five years for some patients and
faded away almost completely a decade after the surgery was performed,
according to a recently completed Department of Veterans Affairs study.

"The benefits of coronary artery bypass surgery . . . . lasted fewer than 11
years," concludes a report appearing in the July issue of the American Heart
Association's scientific journal, <u>Circulation</u>. The authors say their study
was the first large-scale randomized trial designed to evaluate the effect of
bypass surgery compared to medical (drug) therapy for patients with stable
angina pectoris, chest pain due to coronary heart disease.

The blood-vessel grafts used to bypass clogged coronary arteries begin to
get clogged themselves about five to seven years after the surgery, explains
Peter Peduzzi, Ph.D., lead author of the report and assistant chief of the VA
Cooperative Studies Program Coordinating Center in West Haven, Conn.

"The grafts don't stay open forever," says Peduzzi, "and when they begin
to close, the benefits begin to diminish."

Today, physicians use improved surgical techniques as well as better
medicines -- new drugs that reduce heart pain, for example, and drugs that
help keep bypass grafts open longer after the operation, Peduzzi points out.
So today's patients may have fewer problems than those in the VA study.

"To find out what the effect of bypass surgery is today," he says, "you
actually would have to do another trial. Unfortunately, you may have to wait
another 10 or 15 years to get the results."

Coronary artery bypass surgery is the most common operation performed for
angina. The AHA estimates that 392,000 of the procedures were performed in
1990, the most recent year for which statistics are available.

Between 1972 and 1974, the VA trial enrolled 686 male veterans with stable

-more-

FIGURE 1

Circ/Peduzzi/Takaro - 2

angina -- chest pain produced upon exertion because the heart muscle isn't getting enough oxygen-rich blood through disease-narrowed arteries. Patients were randomly assigned to have coronary bypass surgery or to the medical treatment group, who did not receive surgery. However, 154 of the 354 assigned to the medical treatment group later "crossed over" to the surgery group, usually because their chest pain persisted or worsened.

During the first 11 years, patients assigned to the surgery group benefited in terms of survival rates and reduction of chest pain, but the differences between the two groups disappeared entirely by the 18th year of the study, reports Timothy Takaro, M.D., co-author of the study.

"The benefits of surgery don't last forever," says Takaro, the surgeon who served as co-chairman of the VA study and helped organize it in the 1960s. He retired four years ago, after serving as chief of surgery and, later, chief of staff at the Asheville (N.C.) VA Medical Center.

This and other studies suggest that the patients who benefit most from bypass surgery are those with severe coronary artery disease, Takaro points out. In fact, adds Peduzzi, the surgery was most effective in improving survival among VA patients with disease blocking the major artery serving the left ventricle, the heart's main pumping chamber.

"I think the main thing this study shows is that the physician has to be discriminating about the kind of coronary artery disease a patient has," Takaro says. "And it's fair that the physician should inform the patient about the probabilities of survival and how long the good effects of surgery are going to last, if there are to be any."

Many patients request bypass operations because the pain of angina usually is lessened by surgery, adds Takaro, but that benefit "pretty much fades after only five years. There are lots of patients who have mild symptoms and mild disease who probably shouldn't be rushed into surgery," he says.

Most physicians today suggest bypass surgery only for patients with a poor prognosis and for those in whom medical treatments have been unsuccessful, Takaro and Peduzzi say.

Other co-authors are Katherine Detre, M.D., Dr.P.H.; Herbert Hultgren, M.D., and the VA Coronary Artery Bypass Surgery Cooperative Study Group.

Circulation is one of six journals published by the Dallas-based AHA.

#

MEDIA ADVISORY: Dr. Peduzzi can be reached in West Haven at ▮▮▮▮▮▮▮▮▮ ▮▮▮▮▮▮▮ Reporters may call (214) 706-1396 for copies of the report.

hsn/jrnls/752/cl

But Is It News?

Many PR professionals have provided answers to the question "When is a press release news?" Philip Lesly[9] says it's news when it contains one or more of the major ingredients of human interest, such as when it

- Is novel
- Relates to famous persons
- Is directly important to great numbers of people
- Involves conflict
- Involves mystery or crime
- Is considered confidential
- Pertains to the future
- Is romantic or sexy
- Is funny

To test these news qualifications, examine the front page of your daily newspaper. Many of the local and national political pieces reached that newspaper through press releases and press conferences. Also, many of the interviews in the paper were generated by media relations people who "pitched" the idea to the paper.

Those in the PR business call this practice "pitching stories." Stories, or news, are what media relations people have to sell to the media. The effective pitching of a story requires consummate skill. If you're a *Fortune 500* company and you have a dramatic financial turnaround, the job of placing that story is far easier than it might be if you represented a defense contractor cutting jobs.

A major financial story is reported on by the Associated Press and distributed to all its newspapers and broadcast clients for release. The impact of such a story on the financial pages of a major newspaper is far-reaching. It is read by stockholders, brokers, potential investors, customers, dealers, suppliers, employees, and competitors. The feature pages, as well, are typically developed from the pitches of media relations people.

The Exclusivity Factor and Other Woes

Very often it is the media relations person's judgment to "sell" an exclusive story to a newspaper, magazine, or broadcast source. He or she will make it clear on the release itself and in conversation with the reporter or editor that it is exclusive. The media may then elect to go with the story, or reject it if its subject does not warrant coverage beyond a brief mention; in the latter case, the media relations person can submit it as an exclusive to another source or send it out to all the media.

Important newspapers such as the *Wall Street Journal,* the *New York Times,* and the *Washington Post* will often run exclusive pieces. Where a media relations person runs into trouble is when an "exclusive" is pitched to a number of different media sources. In the business that's called "double or triple planting." Most editors deplore it, but others don't care where and how they get their story ideas.

Joel Pomerantz, a veteran PR practitioner, airs the frustrations of media relations people. He decries the "disdainful attitudes" toward PR that some media people harbor.[10]

Some cases in point:

• You suggest to a reporter a story idea involving your client, provide a great deal of background material, and give the writer many leads to flesh out the piece. The article appears without any mention of your client.

• You go to great lengths to make the CEO of an important client company available for an urgently solicited telephone interview that consumes nearly forty-five minutes of his time. The piece runs, incorporating many of his thoughts, but completely without attribution.

• You propose a perishable story to an editor who expresses immediate interest. The editor sits on the proposal for weeks. Nothing happens. Meanwhile, it's too late to pitch it to anyone else.

• You set up a requested interview with a client. She is quoted accurately, but totally out of context, resulting in a damaging, unintended impression.

We counter Pomerantz's plaint with the media person's point of view. Most reliable journalists loathe PR-managed news, that is, the piece with a positive twist or "spin." These writers prefer to originate their own stories based on reportage and research. But of course, this is not always possible because of budget and time considerations. Therefore, the relationship with PR people is often symbiotic—journalists have difficulty working with PR people, yet they can't function without them.

MEDIA CONTACTS

The PR publication *Bulldog Reporter* puts out a directory of contact information on about 2,100 media outlets—newspapers, magazines, TV, and radio stations. PR pros call the directory, *Western Media Contacts,* a "pitch book."

A sample listing in the directory for the Los Angeles bureau chief of the *Wall Street Journal* reads as follows:

> Prefers broad trends in industry, less on a single company. Use a fax only for breaking news stories, not for feature stories or general pitches. Best day to contact him is Friday. Pet peeve: People who send the same pitch to 50 media outlets.

Another listing in *Western Media Contacts* is for the various departments of the *San Francisco Chronicle:*

> The writer of a six-time business column looks for companies to watch, strategies, investment ideas, and new sources. Emphasizes that he is a "tough pitch," but on the other hand, wants to be "inundated" with phone tips (NOT releases). Insists that PR people offer him exclusives.

The noted *San Francisco Chronicle* columnist Herb Caen is also listed:

> Asks that he be called from 3:00–5:30 P.M. for the next day's column, but never on Tuesday. Wants only exclusives.

What is evident from these listings is that a skilled practitioner must know all the reporters' idiosyncrasies. In a sense, he or she must have the insight to penetrate the minds of editors, reporters, and broadcast-news directors. Without these trade secrets, they just won't get "the ink," and that is how to survive in the PR business.

What Clout Is All About

As in any other business or profession, the ability to reach influential people pays off. In advertising, often contacts rather than creativity win new accounts. So it is in PR.

Media relations people at the largest PR counsel firms have clout by virtue of the standing of their clients. It is certainly an accepted practice for an editor to agree to do a piece on Client A in exchange for an exclusive interview with the controversial CEO of Client B.

A media relations person who has established himself or herself as a source—that is, a source of information about a subject, or even as a source of sources—also exercises clout. This cooperation makes an editor's or reporter's job easier and ultimately benefits the PR person.

John Scanlon, a heavyweight New York PR professional, known in the business as an "image-fixer," is a top executive with the Sawyer Miller Group. Scanlon is often asked to repair damaged images. He is successful at it because he's spent thirty years accumulating important friends in the media. It also helps that he's sat on the other side of the desk, both in the business world and in government.

Scanlon has unparalleled access to the power of the press, and this is particularly important when he represents unpopular clients or causes. In one case, he served as PR counsel for the editors of the arch-conservative *Dartmouth Review*, who were suspended from school for harassing a black professor of music whose teaching style and political views they found objectionable. Here, Scanlon functioned as a criminal attorney. He tried to convince the public that the editors' punishment amounted to a violation of their right of free speech.

In another case, Scanlon was called upon to represent Philip Morris and two other cigarette companies. They were jointly defending themselves against a lawsuit brought by a New Jersey man whose wife had died of lung cancer. Their defense was that there is still no proof that heavy smoking is lethal, and that, regardless of the warning on the pack itself, she chose to smoke of her own free will.

Scanlon also represented CBS in a suit against charges that it defamed General William Westmoreland, portraying him as trying to deceive his superiors regarding the size of enemy forces in Vietnam. He represented United Surgical, Inc., which was attacked for demonstrating its patented surgical stapler on live dogs.

Scanlon is able to justify his fee of $250 an hour plus expenses because he delivers. He can immediately reach top columnists, the managing editor of the *New York Times*, ABC's Peter Jennings, CBS's Dan Rather, and NBC's Tom Brokaw. This access doesn't guarantee that his clients will always win, but it certainly assures that they'll get a fair hearing.

STAGING PRESS CONFERENCES AND INTERVIEWS

When the nation's president chooses to have a press conference, there's no problem guaranteeing that it will be well attended. Dozens of domestic and foreign correspondents are *assigned* to the president. They are constantly receiving memoranda and releases from the president's press secretary. A live press conference allows for direct questions to the chief executive.

Similarly, heads of corporations and organizations desire to "meet the press." In this way, their comments and opinions will be transmitted to a wide audience. But press conferences shouldn't be arranged at the drop of a hat. Rather, according to *PR News*, a press conference is warranted only if:

- the news merits the busy reporters' time
- the information cannot be communicated as effectively in writing or by telephone
- it's necessary to tell the story to a number of the media at the same time

- there's genuine interest in the news among a reasonable portion of the general public
- a recognized, respected, and well-prepared spokesperson can be provided
- the announcement can be tied to another timely and newsworthy issue or event
- interesting visual elements are available
- it's required in order to meet competition from other breaking news, such as election coverage or other activities that command attention.

Most of these criteria must be met to stage a successful press conference. (See also Howard Rubenstein's interview in Chapter 5 for his four basic rules regarding press conferences.)

The Interview

A press conference is an interview that offers the media an opportunity to listen to and question one or more individuals on a particular subject or event.

An interview is typically arranged for a client by a PR media relations person. For example, suppose that the CEO of a genetics engineering company is eager to inform the financial community of dramatic new developments. The CEO's PR person must make the decision whether to call a press conference to tell the story to a group of media representatives or to set up an interview with the influential *Wall Street Journal.* If the interview with this publication goes well, it may become a page-one story, with major financial implications for the company.

If the PR person chooses the latter option, much preparation is involved. He or she must first call the publication and pitch the story to a particular reporter—one who covers this kind of story. As an exclusive, the interview becomes more attractive to the reporter.

The next step after a positive initial phone contact is a request by the reporter for a "backgrounder" on the company—that is, a short printed briefing or report providing background information on the company. Next, a place and time for the interview are arranged, either at the CEO's office, or another location.

Prior to the interview, the PR person will brief the CEO on the angles the reporter will be looking for. Good preparation can help make the interview a success. The PR person may attend the interview to offer support for the CEO.

The interview of a book author on network TV shows such as "Today" and "Good Morning America" may result in sales of tens of thousands of copies. However, the author must be able to "sell" the book in only forty or fifty seconds of air time. If he or she doesn't or isn't able to show the cover on camera, that's a significant lost opportunity. The skilled PR practitioner who sets up the interview knows all the tricks and will brief the client/author accordingly.

STAGING A MEDIA OR SPECIAL EVENT

The special event is the most visible of PR strategies. If successful, it exposes a large, visible, and influential audience to a product, an issue, or an individual. Special PR events take many forms, including celebrity appearances, fairs, anniversary celebrations, dedications, conferences and seminars, plant and building dedications, and the like. For the PR person, planning, promoting, and staging a special event is a most demanding function.

Howard R. Mitchell III outlines the elements involved in staging a special event[11]:

- Meeting with clients concerning objectives, deadlines, budgets, and the specific nature of the event
- Compiling target list of attendees
- Producing collateral material such as press kits, displays, and invitations
- Coordinating mailing of invitations
- Coordinating event logistics, speakers, refreshments, exhibits, displays, name tags, parking, security, and like details
- Briefing client, staff, and media
- Coordinating development and production of audio/visual presentations and/or scripts for the event
- Coordinating pre-event publicity

- Providing follow-up
- Analyzing results

Case Study: Mikhail Gorbachev Comes to San Francisco

What could be more stressful than the assignment to handle press relations for a world leader in your own city, with only ten days to do all the planning? An article in *Bulldog Reporter,* July 23, 1990, details the preparation for the event. (Reprinted with permission.)

ULTIMATE PRO BONO? "MIKHAIL GORBACHEV'S COMING TO SF IN 10 DAYS. COULD YOU HANDLE THE PRESS AS A FAVOR?" Those weren't the exact words used by SF chief of protocol **Charlotte Mailliard-Swig,** but **Peter B. Necarsulmer,** founder/pres. of **The PBN Co.,** SF/Sacramento PR/PA consultancy, got the message. And it took him about 10 seconds to say "yes."

Alerting the Media: PBM had to notify global media it was credentialing press for Mikhail Gorbachev's Bay Area visit. Some 2800 media were expected for legit credentials; hundreds more would apply. "We had to fill the vacuum because the mayor's office, Stanford University [a scheduled site], the San Francisco Chamber of Commerce and the White House were swamped with calls," notes Necarsulmer.

PBN got the word out via an advisory through the local wire service bureaus: UPI, Reuters, AP, plus Business Wire and Bay City News Service. The advisory noted PBN was coordinating with U.S. Secret Service, the USSR Consulate General and the SF Mayor's Office, as well as handling media rels for the June 3–4 visit.

Forming Teams: PBN alerted its clients, worked night and day to meet previous client deadlines, then broke up into internal teams: Logistics and Comms., Site Advance, Credentialing, News Bureau. Latter was not in the original game plan, says Necarsulmer, "but it quickly became apparent we'd need news updates, color stuff." (Updates were issued when news was solid and confirmed, rather than released at scheduled times. All copy was in English.)

PBN installed five more faxes at its SF office, termed the "temporary press office" til June 1, and used AT&T's Worldwide fax service to send 500 advisories at a crack.

Credentialing the Press: PBN worked with Sig Rogich, special asst. to Pres. Bush, Tom Harrington, press officer for the Secret Service, and Sergei Aivazian, vice consul for the Soviet Consul General. Scott Shafer and Art Silverman, Mayor Agnos' press secretaries, issued a general credential and event-specific credentials for pool coverage at certain sites. PBN made it clear that U.S. Information Agency/State Dept. or Bush/Gorby summit credentials were no good.

"To take the monkey off our backs," Necarsulmer says, he had local press police and form their own pools for print, photo, TV, radio. The networks relied on local stations for pool coverage.

Some journalists with "real close access" to Bush/Gorby needed "full Secret Service background checks," says Necarsulmer. PBN issued 2,750 credentials, had "excellent cooperation" from everyone, except a few freelance photographers working with photo agencies. One AP shooter "got violent and aggressive" but a PBN staffer notified the AP photo boss, who had seen the antics on TV; the photographer was ousted.

Working with the Soviet Press: The Soviet press corps, 25 strong, essentially spoke no English, was credentialed by the KGB and the Soviet Foreign Ministry when the group got off the plane and checked into the Soviets' HQ—SF's Fairmont Hotel. In short, the Soviet press members were no trouble and proved to be hard workers.

Backgrounders and Updates: PBN's media advisories were simple, direct, chronological, free of hype/propaganda and anything political. They were numbered, dated and had the hour of release. All times were PDT. All directions were clearly spelled out. Fees for hookups to feeds, plus technical step-by-steps were included. Sr. PBN staffers were identified as contacts. Assignments for PBN staffers and volunteers working with the firm were straightforward.

Press kits were compiled and included brochures and backgrounders on Stanford, the Fairmont; lists of Soviet and East European experts, research centers and programs at the univ.; backgrounders on biz services in SF; history of Soviet–American relations. Pool memos had background, Social Security numbers, date of birth, hometown of all members. The written comm. were amazingly comprehensive, yet totally fat-free.

What Did PBN Learn? Agency partners Necarsulmer, Sacco and

Thurman agree the "key to successful pooling is to utilize reporters in the decision-making process. The recipe for suicide is to play Solomon." Next, consult with media in advance on technical requirements. Third, have printed transcripts of all speeches ready an hour before delivery.

Fourth, check with a prior credentialing team to learn from its mistakes. (PBN interviewed people who credentialed press in Minneapolis, Gorbachev's previous stop.) Fifth, all iron-clad schedules will change at the last minute; roll with the punches. Sixth, some White House correspondents will try to bend your rules to suit them; expect some hassle from the warhorses.

Seventh, stay close to the action and don't all stay tethered to a desk/phone. (PBN chartered an RV as its rolling office.) Eighth, make sure your volunteers are pros and not just do-gooders who want something to do. (Jim Caudill, who heads Ketchum PR's biz/fin'l div. in SF, headed a team of three Ketchumites who volunteered.)

Results: "An incredible level of professional satisfaction for every member of the firm," says Necarsulmer, "the pinnacle." What's more, the experience "inspired additional confidence on the part of our clients. They feel good we were given a tough assignment and delivered."

PBN has won some new biz because of its work—Americom Int'l, a joint venture of Radisson Hotels and Intourist, the Soviet tourism agency, retained PBN to open the first Western hotel, complete with biz center, in Moscow in Dec. PBN also has other new biz inquiries and is mulling opening a Moscow office.

What about out-of-pocket costs? They totaled $68,000, but Pacific Telesis and the Swigs, owners of the Fairmont, are heading a fundraising effort to wipe out the debt. —C.B.

Special Events of Special Interest

Special events take many forms, and planning them, of course, requires many different approaches.

The National Air and Space Museum, part of the Smithsonian Institution, creates at least one event a year. On July 20, 1989, it celebrated the twentieth anniversary of the *Apollo 11* moon landing, with a highlight being an outdoor public ceremony at the museum to which U.S. President George Bush, Vice President Dan Quayle, the astronaut crew of *Apollo 11*, high-ranking officials from the Smithsonian and NASA, and scores of VIPs were invited. A late-night "Lunar Landing Party" was staged with actual footage of the Neil Armstrong moon walk shown on closed-circuit monitors around the building.

Planning the event began eighteen months in advance, with regularly scheduled meetings with all departments of the museum participating. Early planning also involved negotiations with officials at NASA, whose primary interest was maximum public relations impact.

For the communications staff of the Smithsonian, the hard work paid off. Press coverage was extensive, with a total of seventy-five camera crews covering the event for local and network TV. In addition to the media exposure, the event enhanced the museum's image. It also produced good will and a spirit of community among the local participating groups. The event gave the Smithsonian staff members a feeling of pride and confidence in the Institution. For the public, the event provided an educational, family-oriented, festive happening.

Arranging a Press Tour

One of the major assignments of media relations people is the press tour. It is used when a movie star goes on tour to promote a new movie or when a celebrity goes on a tour to promote a new product bearing his or her name. Tours are used extensively in book publishing when authors are sent on the road to hustle sales for their books.

An extensive author's tour may consist of five to ten interviews a day with print, radio, and TV media in fifteen or twenty cities over a period of three weeks. In addition to the interviews, there are often signings in bookstores. Pity the poor author who has to hear his or her own spiel a hundred times.

When a celebrity author is involved, a PR person always accompanies the author. It's equally trying on that person, who has to shepherd the author and handle all the arrangements.

Figure 2 shows a listing for an author's tour. We reprint it courtesy of *ABA Newswire*.[12]

Tours such as this are arranged by the publicity departments of

Jay Kordich, **THE JUICEMAN'S POWER OF JUICING,** Morrow, $15.00, pub date 4/20/92, ISBN 0-668-11443-1. (Tour by Jericho Promotions)

NATIONAL

Print:

People

USA Today

New York Times (4/15)

Newsweek (4/21)

Associated Press feature (4/20)

Forbes author profile (3/2/92)

Self interview & book profile (5/92)

Family Circle (7/92)

M. Inc. interview & book profile (5/92)

Practical Gourmet book review (5/92)

Woman's Day: Lose Weight/Stay Healthy issue (Summer 1992)

Men's Health interview & book profile (Summer 1992)

Cooking Light review (8/92)

Ironman review (8/92)

Your Health interview & book profile (Summer 1992)

Fitness feature

TV:

CNN (4/27)

Fox National News (4/17)

700 Club (5/27)

Radio:

Food Show • indep. syn. (5/4)

USA Radio Network (820 stations, 5/26)

Master Control • Southern Baptist Radio, ABC Radio & 700 stations

PORTLAND - 4/27

Signing & Demo: Meier & Frank

Good Morning • KXYQ-FM

Fan Forum • KFXX-AM

Sunday Radio Magazine • KEX-AM

SEATTLE - 4/28

Signing: Pipeline

Seattle Times interview (4/8)

Northwest Afternoon • KOMO-TV (tape)

WCKG-FM

SAN FRANCISCO - 4/29

KPOO Radio

LOS ANGELES - 4/30

Signing & Demo: Broadway

Peter Tilden • KABC-TV

KBRT-AM interview (tape)

Talk of the Town • Simmons Cable TV (live)

Los Angeles Times

Jackie Olden • KGIL-AM

World of Cookbooks

SAN DIEGO - 5/1

Signing & Demo: Robinson's

Noon News • KFMB-TV

Inside San Diego • KGTV-TV (tape)

Roger Hedgecock Morning Show • KDSO-AM

Issues and Answers • KIFM-FM (tape)

LAS VEGAS - Week of 5/4

Signing & Demo: Dillards

Appearance & signing: Kathy's Gourmet Store

Good Morning Las Vegas • KTNV-TV (ABC)

AM Southern Nevada • KVVU-TV (FOX)

First Step w/Ed Bernstein • KVBC-TV (NBC)

Morning Drive • KWNR-FM

DENVER - 5/11

Signing: Tattered Cover

Demo: May D & F

Good Afternoon Colorado • KUSA-TV (1 live, 1 tape)

Morning News • KUSA-TV (ABC)

NASHVILLE - 5/12

Signing: David Kidd

Morning Show • WGFX-FM

CLEVELAND - 5/13

Signing: Booksellers

Morning Exchange • WEWS-TV

Noon News • WJW-TV

Morning Drive • WWWE-AM

Morning Drive • WLTF-FM

Community Spotlight • WELW-AM

TAMPA - 5/14

Waldenbooks & More

Newswatch 8 at Noon • WFLA-TV

MIAMI - 5/15

Burdine's

Live at 11:00 • WTVJ-TV

DETROIT - 5/18

Cargo Express

Noon News • WJBK-TV

Warren Pierce • WJR-AM

PITTSBURGH - 5/20

Signing & Demo: Kaufmann's

Pittsburgh Press

Morning Magazine • KDKA-AM

ATLANTA - 5/21

Signing: Waldenbooks

Noon News • WXIA-TV

Hello Georgia • WXIA-TV

Talk of the Town • WTLK-TV

PHOENIX - 5/22

Signing: Barnes & Noble

Contact Arizona • KXEG-AM

DALLAS - 5/26

Signing & Demo: Dillards

News • USA Radio Network

Master Control • Southern Baptist Radio

VIRGINIA BEACH - 5/27

700 Club • CBN Network

BOSTON - 5/28

Signing: Lauriat's

People Are Talking • WBZ-TV

HOUSTON - 5/29

Signing & Demo: Foley's

Morning Drive • KSEV-AM

Morning Drive • KHMX-FM

FIGURE 2

book publishers. In addition to these in-house publicity staffs, publishers often hire PR firms that specialize in tours. In some cases, local PR firms are engaged to supplement the efforts of the publisher.

O. J. Simpson, erstwhile football star turned sports commentator, was known to sports fans as "The Juice." Today's candidate for that colorful appellation is Jay Kordich, "The Juiceman." Starting as a TV pitchman promoting the nutritional value of juices, Kordich is now a media personality and of course has written a book.

Note the extensive author's tour "The Juiceman's" publisher, William Morrow, organized for the book's introduction in April 1992— nineteen cities in thirty-two days. In addition to the trip, the author did interviews that resulted in fourteen newspaper and magazine stories. The feature in the Associated Press may have resulted in pickup by hundreds of newspapers.

So important is this tour for Kordich's publisher, it employed a publicity and tour management firm, Jericho Promotions, to handle arrangements.

Because of last-minute schedule changes on the part of the media, book publicity people often have only a month to coordinate their bookings. They must make hundreds of phone calls to line up appearances. They keep accurate, up-to-date card files on the personnel lists of TV and radio interview shows and publications that interview authors. To help make the "sell," publicity people send the media a copy of the book to be promoted along with a press release. Final arrangements are usually made by phone.

Typically, one senior person at a publisher will handle one book, with a junior person assisting when the tour is extensive. For a limited tour, a junior publicity person may be responsible for the entire effort.

A Creative Media Opportunity

In the early 1970s, when I was publishing the *National Lampoon,* we were a hot item. Everything we did was news, whether we contrived it or not. We also received a large volume of "fan" mail, from an assortment of crazies, racists, and even ordinary citizens who hated the magazine.

One day a package about 6″ × 9″ arrived in the mail. Our mail-person didn't think that was so unusual; we received many packages. But this one was different—it was ticking.

Seizing the moment, one of our editors immediately called the bomb squad of the New York City Police Department, the three networks, wire services, the *New York Times,* and the *Daily News.* To the press he said in a panicked voice, "This is the *National Lampoon,* and we've just received a bomb. Come quickly."

Within minutes they all arrived—the police with their specially padded bomb wagon, the media with their cameras. It didn't take the police long to detect that the ticking "bomb" was actually an alarm clock. That night on the 11 o'clock news all three local news shows carried the episode, including an interview with a *Lampoon* editor. No, the event had not been planned. But it made for a short, humorous news feature, with even some doubt over its legitimacy.

Collecting and Analyzing Media Coverage

Most large corporations and organizations that conduct PR programs subscribe to clipping services. These services provide clippings of all press mentions of their organization. Media relations people live in a constant quest for this "ink." Yet the sheer volume of clippings does not determine the effectiveness of a media relations program.

Sophisticated organizations use market research techniques to measure the results of their public relations efforts. These measures include focus groups; motivation research telling how the public feels about a company; effectiveness surveys that measure the impact of a company's PR activities on the target audience(s); and a PR audit, a wide-ranging study that explores a company's PR activities, both internally and externally.

Media relations is the most significant function of PR. It offers a challenging career.

CHAPTER 9

Employee Publications
and
Employee Relations

The preparation of employee publications is an important component of an organization's total PR program. The concept of employee publications has been around for more than sixty years and today has reached a high degree of specialization.

The primary role of employee publications is to boost morale. But, in a larger sense, they do more. Company publications tell employees:

- how well the company is doing in the marketplace
- where the company is headed and how it is going to get there
- how employees fit in with these plans
- what technological developments have occurred within the company and industry
- the status of labor–management issues.

Typically, company publications emanate from the corporate employee communications department. A permanent staff of editors, writers, and designers is responsible for these publications. At times, freelance writers are used.

Many large companies publish multiple employee publications targeted to specific audiences within the organization. AT&T even publishes a daily newsletter available on seventy-five electronic mail networks within the company. Recipients post paper copies for co-workers who don't have computers.

EXAMPLES OF EMPLOYEE PUBLICATIONS

In 1982, at General Motors' Automotive Components Group in Saginaw, Michigan, management research uncovered "a lack of trust between management and labor, poor communications throughout the division, decision making limited to a handful, minimum employee involvement, and unpredictable leadership." Ron Actis, then director and sole employee of the public affairs department, with the cooperation of top management, was determined to improve the Saginaw division's negative image among employees.

A number of programs were instituted, including face-to-face discussions between supervisors and employees and a complete overhaul of the division's employee publications. Today, Actis is group director of communications and public affairs for the Saginaw division, with a staff of twelve. His program has been a success. Management and labor interaction has vastly improved employee relations, and there is a comprehensive network of employee publications geared to specific audiences.

A single-page publication, the *Daily Newsletter,* is distributed to 20,000 employees. It consists of news about the Saginaw division and, to a lesser extent, articles about the entire auto industry and the parent company, General Motors (GM). In addition, a 6-page monthly tabloid, *Steering Columns,* is mailed to every employee's and retiree's home. A bimonthly newsletter, *Report to Supervisors,* is distributed to 3,000 managers and supervisors. *Joint Activities,* a quarterly newsletter, is written and funded by GM and the United Auto Workers. And there are three other publications.

What we see here is a progressive approach to the improvement of employee relations—the use of company publications to reach employees with specialized information.

IBM's *THINK* is a class act. This monthly publication, in existence since 1934, has a circulation of 400,000 in 138 countries. A recent issue had 64 pages and was printed almost totally in four colors on fine paper stock. But what is most impressive about *THINK* is its provocative editorial content and sparkling graphics.

Thousands of these publications are published by large corporations and by smaller companies as well. They offer an excellent place to get started in PR and to develop one's writing skills.

EMPLOYEE RELATIONS

At many large corporations, employee relations is a province of the PR and public affairs department. Almost every large company is active in this area.

In his book *Innovative Employee Communication: New Approaches to Improving Trust, Teamwork and Performance,* Alvie T. Smith highlights some outstanding programs.[13] Here are a few:

- Ford Motor Company uses satellite TV as part of a multimedia system for communications with its 360,000 employees and management groups.
- Federal Express beams original informational programs via a satellite TV system to its 85,000 employees in more than 1,100 locations in North America, Great Britain, and other parts of Europe.
- IBM uses print, videotapes, and satellite TV to reach its 200,000 employees. Its "Speak Up" communication program has generated more than 300,000 letters in the past thirty years.

In a campaign that won an award from the Public Relations Society of America, Bank of America, which has had a dramatic financial resurgence in recent years, in 1989 awarded 50,000 employees with 10 shares of stock each. The cost to the company: $20 million. The bank paid the initial federal and state withholding taxes on the awards and granted an extra vacation day for each employee as well.

The bank's employees were delighted with the gift, and thousands sent letters of appreciation to the bank's chairman, Tom Clausen. Employees even called local papers to bring attention to this most practical award. Perhaps there's no correlation, but in 1989 Bank of America had the best year in its history.

CHAPTER 10

Speechwriting

One-third of *Fortune 250* companies have a "chief executive speechwriter" whose main responsibility is writing speeches for CEOs.[14] More significantly, these are power jobs. At least half of these top speechwriters earn at least $90,000 per year, with a median at $75,000.

The clout and prestige come from being close to the top rungs of management. In a sense, these chief speechwriters act as advisers to their bosses.

Before you rush off to take Speechwriting 101, let us remind you that not all speechwriters write for CEOs. Some are considered mid-level people and write speeches for lesser folk for less money.

Chief executive speechwriters spend an average of fifty hours on a major address—of which twenty hours are spent on research and fifteen on the first draft—and prepare an average of thirty speeches per year. What do speechwriters do with the rest of their time? Often they ghostwrite bylined articles for executives for the trade and consumer press and the investment community.

Speechwriting is a creative craft. Some CEOs and top executives choose to speak from an outline rather than from a prepared script. Doing so frees the executive from having to read every word. He or she can instead concentrate on motivating the audience. The speechwriter's preparation is no less intense.

The speechwriter must be able to write the way one speaks, not the way one writes to be read. And although the speechwriter cannot instill dynamism in a speaker with a dull voice and presentation, he or she can sprinkle a speech with enough humor and spice to make it listenable.

A problem the speechwriter faces from time to time is the lack of access to the CEO and the other top executives he or she is writing for. Often these people are shielded by overzealous underlings who perhaps regard the speechwriter as a threat to their power.

The Executive Speaker is an excellent newsletter for speakers and speechwriters.[15] Reading this publication, you become aware of the nuances and techniques in the craft of speechwriting. For example, a recent issue stressed the importance of "openings" in attracting the audience's interest and attention. It quoted a Groucho Marx introduction: "Before I speak, I have something important to say."

Wittiness and conciseness are key attributes of good speeches. *The Executive Speaker* illustrates this with the following excerpt:

> Presenters (speechmakers) would do well to remember when adapting their goals to their group what the Reverend William Sloane Coffin said about the length of an effective sermon, "No souls are saved after twenty minutes."

The Executive Speaker also serves as a clearinghouse for speechwriters and speakers, providing information about books, seminars and workshops, video and audio cassettes, and a reference file of more than 3,500 speeches.

RESEARCHING THE SPEAKING EVENT

The speechwriter must research the event thoroughly. One speech-writing professional has a checklist of twenty-five pieces of information he needs to know before he writes a speech. These include:

- Will the speaker stay behind the lectern or will he or she wander among the audience?
- What is the male-to-female and minority composition of the audience?
- What is the audience's attitude toward the corporation or group?
- What is the physical setup of the room in which the speech will take place?

Timothy J. Koranda, a veteran speechwriter, sums it up: "Speech-writing is a personal service like psychiatry. And like a psychiatrist, the speechwriter needs to know what's on the chairman's mind. Ideally, the speechwriter should report directly to the chairman and be his or her alter ego."[16]

CAREER TIP:
HOW TO BECOME A SPEECHWRITER

1. Listen to the great speaker/motivators: Jesse Jackson, Robert Schuller, Mario Cuomo, Billy Graham, Ann Richards. Focus on their content, structure, and style.

2. Watch ordinary people make speeches. Listen to the subject matter, and evaluate.

3. Attend speechwriting forums. They're held in dozens of cities, including Boston, Detroit, Minneapolis, Houston, Chicago, and Washington, D.C. The local club of PR professionals will know the dates.

4. Volunteer to write a speech for a local political group or charitable organization.

5. Network with the chief speechwriter in your organization. Go through the steps he or she takes when writing a speech.

6. Invent a topic and write a speech about it—say, a speech your CEO will make to a group of Japanese businessmen interested in investing in your industry.

7. Read all you can about speechwriting and speechmaking. Two good books are Peggy Noonan's *What I Saw at the Revolution* and Richard Goodwin's *Remembering America*. Noonan wrote speeches for Presidents Ronald Reagan and George Bush; Goodwin was an adviser to and speechwriter for John F. Kennedy and Lyndon Johnson.

CHAPTER 11

Issues Management and Public Affairs

Before 1950 the area of corporate public affairs barely existed. In the past forty-plus years, however, public affairs has proliferated to a point where most large corporations maintain extensive staffs. What is the reason for this growth? The answer lies in the need for business to monitor, evaluate, predict, and influence the political environment.

Many people with a political science background are attracted to this field, as are former congressional and federal aides who basically function as lobbyists. Public affairs positions exist within both corporations and PR firms.

Although there are many titles for these specialists, their basic task involves lobbying and gathering intelligence on the activities of federal and state legislative and executive bodies and regulatory agencies. At the top rung of this ladder, public affairs people are very highly paid.

One large PR firm, Ruder Finn, highlights its public affairs services. It sums up the role of public affairs as follows:

• Research, write, and print congressional testimony, press releases, and lobbying support materials

• Analyze issues, including various proposed and existing legislation and regulations

• Arrange face-to-face meetings with members of Congress, regulators, commissioners, key staff members, and administrators.

The Public Affairs Council is a Washington-based membership group of more than 400 companies and noncorporate organizations that seeks to advance the practice of public affairs. It has provided us with an outline of the responsibilities of a public affairs department.

POLITICAL ACTION

Political action committees	Grassroots activities
Political education	Communication on political issues

ISSUES MANAGEMENT

Issues identification
Issues analysis
Responses

COMMUNITY INVOLVEMENT/CORPORATE RESPONSIBILITY

Community relations	Social responsibility programs
Philanthropy	Volunteerism

GOVERNMENT RELATIONS

Federal
State
Local

INTERNATIONAL

Monitoring international socio-political developments	Host-country government relations
	Risk assessment/responses

STRATEGIC PLANNING

Socio-political monitoring
Identification of emerging
 issues

Inputs to business and strategic
plans

COMMUNICATIONS

Media relations
Employee communications
Public relations

From this list one can readily understand the complexity and diversity of the field of public affairs. Issues management, for example, takes place in a number of arenas: federal and state issues, social trends, economic analyses, and international events. Community involvement concerns itself with the broad field of public-interest programs.

Few corporations employ specialists in all of these areas. Many rely on outside PR firms for this expertise. In a smaller company, a single public affairs officer may serve as a one-person lobbyist, issues specialist, regulatory analyst, and media relations specialist, at the same time keeping abreast of all public-policy issues.

THE FUNCTIONS OF COMMUNITY INVOLVEMENT AND CORPORATE RESPONSIBILITY

Let's look at the community involvement area of public affairs. At the corporation or private foundation, support for the arts and educational institutions is the responsibility of the public affairs department. On the receiving end, universities, museums, music and cultural centers, and even zoos have public affairs officers whose functions may include fund raising from governments, foundations, corporations, and individual donors.

With reduced spending on the arts by government and business in the early 1990s, the role of public affairs officers has widened to include increased fund raising from individuals to take up the slack. Often this effort involves direct marketing campaigns. Key to the success of these fund-raising efforts are public-awareness programs to communicate to the various publics just what the institution does and how it does it.

An example of the creative use of PR in these campaigns is the effort of the JBSpeed Museum in Louisville, Kentucky, reported in *PR Journal.*[17] To attract families to visit the museum it ran a special exhibit on the art of the children's favorite character Babar, called "Babar Comes to Life at the Speed." Special bookmarks, good for one free adult admission to the museum, were distributed to schools. In addition, TV spots and billboards promoted the museum's permanent collection and urged viewers to "Peek in on your Picasso" and "Rally 'round your Rubens."

THE ROLE OF THE LOBBYIST

The word "lobbying" derives from the practice of individuals' congregating outside legislative chambers (in the lobby) and attempting to solicit or influence the votes of members of a legislative body on behalf of a group's special interest.

The National Rifle Association is a powerful organization headquartered in Washington, D.C., with the single-issue orientation of opposing legislation that would restrict the use of guns by hobbyists. To achieve this objective, the NRA engages in a sophisticated campaign directed at legislators and their staffs, as well as at the general public. The individual orchestrating this effort is a lobbyist—often a former legislator or government official.

The tools of a lobbyist are action or advocacy kits, position papers, media kits, the staging of media briefings and editorial conferences, and, of course, a strong contact base.

A recent book on the subject offers some of the vernacular of the lobbyist.[18] A "horse" is the legislator persuaded to take the responsibility for one's issue and "pull one's wagon" through the legislative process.

Lobbying is used at the local, state, and federal levels. Washington is the home base for hundreds of organizations whose primary function is lobbying. Politically, they range across the spectrum from liberal groups such as Americans for Democratic Action, the American Civil Liberties Union, and Planned Parenthood to the Conservative Caucus and the National Right to Life Committee on the right.

But lobbying inside the Beltway is hardly limited to organizations with a particular political or social bent. Industry groups also maintain offices in Washington to lobby for their special interests. Examples of these are the American Trucking Association, the American Council of Life Insurance, the Chemical Manufacturers Association, the American Public Power Association, and the National Coal Association.

THE DIVERSITY OF PUBLIC AFFAIRS

The Public Affairs Council publishes an annual report that lists the components of today's public affairs programs. The list illustrates the diversity of this field. Here are some examples:

- Communication tools
- Corporate contributions
- International public affairs
- Lobbying regulation
- Local government relations
- Political action committees
- Social responsibility/corporate involvement
- Voter registration programs

Public affairs jobs offer high salaries, excellent opportunities for advancement, and the chance to interact with top management and public officials on the molding of policy.

CHAPTER 12

Public Interest,
Public Service,
Image Building

Corporations engage in public-service programs for a variety of reasons. They find that it is good business to put their best foot forward, to bring to the attention of their various publics an image of quality, social consciousness, and responsibility. They achieve this objective in a number of ways.

Following are examples of programs conducted by large corporations.

PHILIP MORRIS AND THE ARTS

A four-color ad in *Washington Journalism Review*[19] shows a young girl looking at a painting by a black artist, part of a traveling exhibition that goes to Dallas, Atlanta, Milwaukee, and Richmond, Virginia. The ad's headline: "HALLELUJAH. Black art makes a joyful noise to all the land." Its theme: the talents of African-Americans enrich us all, in enterprise as well as the arts. At the bottom of the ad in straight type (i.e., no logos), Philip Morris lists its companies— PM USA, Kraft General Foods, Miller Brewing Company, and the Mission Viejo Company.

Another ad in the series features Philip Morris's sponsorship of the 50th Anniversary Tour of the American Ballet Theatre, and still another, its sponsorship of an exhibition of twentieth-century Russian artist Kazimir Malevich at the National Gallery in Washington. One cannot fault Philip Morris's commitment to the arts. In New York City, their headquarters, it maintains a permanent art gallery.

Diversity marks Philip Morris's public-service programs. An ad in *Washington Journalism Review* talks about its support for STRIVE, a program to reduce unemployment in inner-city neighborhoods. It is significant that this series of ads appeared in the *WJR*, reaching professional journalists. Philip Morris, constantly skirting legislation against cigarette advertising, is eager to convey to the media a good corporation citizen image.

AT&T'S PUBLIC-SERVICE ACTIVITY

The AT&T Foundation is the primary vehicle for the company's philanthropy. Funded with $126 million, it is among the largest endowed corporate foundations in the world. AT&T's public-service program, supported by the Foundation, is active in education, health and social action, and arts and culture. A major component of these activities is the participation of AT&T employees.

In Los Angeles, the AT&T Foundation supports Children Now, a group that provides education and information to teenage parents. In Chicago, AT&T employees work with the city on school reform, and in San Francisco they have become advocates with other corporations and within the community for greater education on the impact of AIDS.

Foundation grants provide support for performing arts centers, orchestras, and theaters around the country. There is even an AT&T Dance Tour, the first corporate-funded program specifically to support dance touring. In education, AT&T channels its contributions in the form of scholarships and grants to colleges and universities.

In terms of structure within the company, AT&T's senior vice president of PR serves as the chairperson, and the vice president of PR acts as president of their foundation's board of trustees. Eight executives serve as officers and managers of the specific programs.

OTHER COMPANIES' PUBLIC-SERVICE PROGRAMS

Programs for Minorities

The 26 million African-Americans represent a $140 billion consumer market. Many corporations are reaching this audience with a straight product appeal as well as through well-thought-out public-service programs.

The Carnation Company sponsors a campaign called Black Dimensions in American History and Black Dimensions in Contemporary American Music. American Airlines publishes a *Travel Guide to Black Conventions and Conferences*. Greyhound runs a Woman of the Year campaign in black-oriented newspapers.

General Electric has established a foundation with a number of academic and cultural programs benefiting minorities and the disadvantaged. Faculty for the Future is designed to increase the number of underrepresented minorities and women who earn their doctorates in engineering, chemistry, physics, and business management from U.S. institutions. GE's College Bound program is attempting to double the number of college-bound students from selected poor and inner-city schools in communities where GE plants are located. It also includes the Elfun Challenge Grant, wherein GE employees and retirees are active as volunteer mentors and tutors.

Opera Broadcasts on Radio

In 1990, the Texaco Company completed fifty years of radio sponsorship of Saturday broadcasts of the Metropolitan Opera. These popular programs are carried on hundreds of stations and reach millions of people. The broadcasts are now even international. Support of the arts is an excellent image builder.

Arts Sponsorships

By sponsoring quality TV programming, the Hallmark Company engages in image building for its company name. IBM and Philip Morris maintain art galleries at their respective headquarters in New York City.

Community Charities

Community relations programs are linked to image building. They bring the corporation's name in front of the public in a positive sense. Corporations conduct their community relations by supporting local communities, poverty programs, minority programs, health care and cultural activities, and charitable contributions. The desired result— the molding of a positive corporate image.

Some examples: McDonald's has for years been supporting the Ronald McDonald Houses, which aid families of critically ill children during their hospital stays. At the Scott Paper Company, community relations is paired with a program of targeted corporate social investment. It even created a product line, "Helping Hand," which is designed both to assist charity and to gain profitable sales volume for the company.

What conclusions can we draw from the examples of the public-interest and public-service programs we have discussed? Certainly these companies and hundreds of others participate in them because they regard doing so as good business. Perhaps they even regard this positive image building as a balance against criticism about a corporation's environmental policy or some future negative occurrence such as a strike or an accident. And, of course, many of these public-interest and public-service programs are tax-deductible.

As a career source, public service and public interest are rewarding areas in the whole field of public relations. They may be less stressful than media relations and crisis management. They may pay less, but they pose a challenging career choice that can be pursued at many levels—corporate, not-for-profit, or governmental.

CHAPTER 13

Strategic Corporate PR and Integrated Communications

In defining the function of strategic corporate PR we need first to define the terms "reactive" and "proactive." When a corporation faces a crisis and then reacts to that crisis by making certain moves, its actions are reactive. In proactive planning, the corporation prepares a crisis program in advance and is then able to control the crisis situation by acting on the strategy of its prearranged plan.

Paul Forbes broadens the objectives of strategic management to the ability of an organization to deal with crises and to "identify its long-term opportunities and threats, mobilize its assets to address them, and carry out a successful implementation strategy."[20]

Carrying out such a program involves six steps, which Forbes articulates as follows:

- scanning the future
- building scenarios for this contingency planning
- reviewing the mission of the organization on an ongoing basis

- setting objectives, strategies, and policies as to where the organization wants to go and how to get there
- implementing this strategy
- evaluating and updating the plan annually.

Forbes sums up strategic planning as "what you do now to bring about a future result."

Following are some practical uses of PR for strategic marketing purposes in the pharmaceutical industry.[21]

- Ciba-Geigy used Mickey Mantle as a celebrity spokesman for its arthritis drug Voltaren. Mantle, known to have arthritis, successfully participated in the clinical trials for the drug. The campaign using Mantle drew 2,000 phone calls in the first 320 days. Even though Voltaren was a late entry into the field, it soon became number two in its category.

- In 1989 Upjohn, recognizing that Hispanic Americans were at higher risk for diabetes than other groups, set up with the American Diabetes Association a special screening program for Hispanics. It screened more than 2,000 potential diabetics, who were then referred to doctors. Upjohn is a leader in oral anti-diabetes therapy. The company can't guarantee that doctors will prescribe their therapy, but by organizing the screening and identifying the potential, they have fulfilled a social need and provided a business opportunity at the same time.

- In 1991, the American Medical Association, representing 250,000 of the nation's doctors, kicked off a major advertising and PR program to portray doctors in a more favorable light. This move was taken to counteract a growing perception on the part of the public that doctors were a bunch of insensitive money-grubbers.

The AMA launched this effort after examining the results of a Gallup poll which showed that 69 percent of the people questioned thought that "people are beginning to lose faith in their doctors." Another phase of the AMA's campaign was to get doctors more involved in community affairs. In this campaign, advertising and PR were closely linked.

INTEGRATED COMMUNICATIONS

Integrated communications brings a number of disciplines under one umbrella. Public relations, advertising, direct marketing, and promotion are coordinated through a single planning system. Implementation of this planning finds PR professionals in the same room with ad agency people to achieve their objectives; that is, to deliver the right messages to the right people through the right medium to elicit the desired response.

When Public Relations Meets Advertising

Perhaps the best way of interpreting integrated communications is by example. James Foster documents a case involving a major bank.[22]

Chicago's Continental Bank repositioned itself in 1988 from its status as a consumer bank to a business bank. As such, the bank relied on corporate executives, money managers, and institutional investors for its financial prosperity. How did Continental implement this integrated communications program?

The company brought its advertising and PR agencies together to draw up a plan that would use advertising and PR to distribute its message to key audiences.

First came an aggressive advertising campaign selling the bank's services to corporations, institutional investors, and wealthy individuals. This was followed by a joint study of corporate competitiveness by Continental and the *Wall Street Journal,* supporting the bank's ad message that it knows corporate America's financing needs.

To reinforce its new image as a business bank, Continental produces an elegant quarterly publication, with articles by CEOs, business school academics, and lawmakers on various economic and business subjects. The bank distributes the journal to a wide group of business prospects. Its sponsorship of the journal creates for Continental a strong association with the financial community.

How an Integrated Communications Campaign
Dealt with an Important Safety Issue

The Genie Company, a successful manufacturer of automatic garage door openers, by 1989 realized the potential danger of these openers, particularly for children. Genie took the radical step of *asking* the government to regulate the industry. By taking a proactive stance on this issue, the company was instrumental in the enactment of federal and state legislation regulating garage door opener safety.

Genie used an integrated PR and advertising program to achieve its objective. The PR phase was designed to highlight the safety issue, and direct mail and advertising were used to reinforce the message.

Bennett S. Rubin, Genie's vice president of marketing and sales, details the steps in the campaign, which was launched in early spring 1990[23]:

• A safety brochure/poster with the theme "Genie Says Safety Is More Than Magic" was produced and offered free to consumers.

• Press kits containing the brochure and a news release were distributed to more than 150 major daily newspapers.

• An article providing safety tips, written by a Genie engineer, was distributed to newspapers across the country.

• The company engaged in a public affairs effort aimed at state and federal legislators to enact legislation on garage door opener safety.

• Genie's dealers were given free infrared noncontact reversing devices with each garage-door opener stocked in order to encourage customers to buy this safety-oriented product.

• A series of ads stressing garage door opener safety were run in daily newspapers, regional city magazines, and large-circulation magazines.

Genie's integrated communications plan was clearly a success. It established the company as a concerned citizen, and in the long run it will sell more garage door openers.

We see here two efforts that combine advertising, research, and PR. These activities are the essence of a sound integrated communications plan.

CHAPTER 14

Financial PR

Bristol-Myers Squibb Company is a giant corporation with total annual sales of about $10 billion. As a result of Bristol-Myers's recent acquisition of the Squibb company, it is a major force in the pharmaceutical business. In fact, thirteen of its drug products generate more than $100 million in annual sales. In late 1990 the company gained FDA approval for the cholesterol-lowering drug Pravastatin. The stakes were high. High cholesterol is a factor in cardiovascular disease, the leading cause of death in most of the developed world, and successful cholesterol-lowering drugs may have worldwide sales of more than $500 million a year.

As soon as the FDA approval came through, Bristol-Myers Squibb's PR people publicized this development to media around the world. The in-house staff was assisted in this assignment by the company's outside PR counsel. Because the introduction of the drug may affect the company's earnings, its financial PR organization was charged with the responsibility of telling the story to its financial publics.

Who are Bristol-Myers Squibb's financial publics? A list of those individuals and groups "whose attention is sought," our earlier definition of a public, includes the following:

- the financial press
- present BMS stockholders
- institutional investors
- mutual fund owners
- brokers
- investment counselors and services
- the investing public
- security analysts
- investment bankers
- commercial bankers
- trustees of estates

Although Bristol-Myers Squibb could not reach all of these publics directly, it could reach some of the most important ones. For example, its hundreds of thousands of present stockholders were informed of the development in a page of the Third Quarter 1990 Report mailed to each of them.

A typical Bristol-Myers Squibb stockholder will read his or her quarterly and annual reports. The development of a major new drug is important financial news. It doesn't mean that the stockholder will immediately decide to buy more of the company's stock, but it does show that Bristol-Myers Squibb's huge research and development expenditures are paying off.

In addition to sending out the quarterly report to stockholders, Bristol-Myers Squibb also mails it to security analysts at brokerage companies and mutual funds. What is it trying to accomplish?

Here's one possible scenario: A security analyst at a large brokerage company receives the quarterly report and a press release about a new drug. On the basis of this information, the analyst telephones the company's financial PR staff, reevaluates the company, and sends out a buy recommendation to all the brokerage firm's customers.

The daunting task of communicating with the press on financial matters for a large corporation is the assignment of the financial media relations department. At IBM a senior corporate media relations executive and his or her staff are responsible for all information requests, interviews, press releases, and printed material regarding financial subjects. These matters include earnings, board of directors' issues, stockholder meetings, production demand and volume, security analysts, and proxy issues.

THE ANNUAL REPORT

Time Warner: The Razzle-dazzle Approach to Annual Reports

In 1989 Time, a giant in magazines and cable television, merged with another giant, Warner Communications, to form a colossus, Time Warner, the world's leading media and entertainment company. The combined company had total revenues in 1991 of $12.021 billion. As a result of the cost of the merger, the company also had long-term debt of $8.7 billion.

It is said that the average reader spends barely 300 seconds reading an annual report. In this brief period the reader is expected to flip through the report's pages and quickly get the gist of a company's unique story. Time Warner's 1991 Annual Report dares the reader to put it down in five minutes. It is a piece of financial show business in the sense that it entertains while at the same time it details the company's solid financial performance.

Time Warner's 1991 Annual Report, designed by the Los Angeles and New York communications agency Frankfurt Gips Balkind, is a striking showcase of its activities. Right from the start, the report's cover sets the tone for its basic theme: Time Warner provides global leadership for its "brands," which include *People, Fortune,* and *Sports Illustrated* magazines; Warner Bros. Pictures; HBO; Atlantic and Elektra music companies; and Lorimar television.

Inside the report numerous four-color graphics illustrate the highlights of Time Warner's year. For example, a color photo of Paul Simon in concert has a caption noting that Simon is a Warner Bros. Records artist who put on a free concert in New York City's Central

Park that was attended by 750,000. It also notes that the concert was carried live by HBO (Time Warner) and released as an album and video. This event contributed to Time Warner's image as a concerned partner in New York City. At the same time, the concert was good business since Time Warner benefited financially.

Is the effect of this annual report just so much razzle-dazzle? Perhaps. After all, stockholders and security analysts are mainly interested in the bottom line. Yet, if you are an overseas film company planning to make a deal with Time Warner, the annual report serves the company by clearly reinforcing its position as the world's largest media organization.

Annual Reports Come of Age

The Securities and Exchange Commission (SEC) sets the guidelines for annual reports. Certain basic financial information and disclaimers must be included. These guidelines have been mandated for the protection of stockholders. However, companies have increasingly used their annual reports for image-building purposes and to strategically position a company in a particular direction.

What we have also seen in reports is an active effort by corporations to show their responsibility in terms of global and environmental issues. As one designer of annual reports put it, "Companies are now using annual reports to try to answer questions before the questions are asked."[24]

In terms of disclosure, companies are choosing candor instead of cant. In its letter to shareholders, Reynolds Metals Company CEO William O. Bourke said, "From a business standpoint, 1991 is a year we are glad to have behind us." Capital Cities/ABC, Inc.,'s CEO and president, in its 1991 annual report, commented on the subject of reduced advertiser spending: "It is not possible at this writing to predict with any confidence when this downturn will be reversed."

Who Does What on an Annual Report

Philip Morris, the nation's largest advertiser, is a company with annual sales of almost $50 billion. Its annual report is a sixty-page publication beautifully printed on high-quality paper with profuse use of color photography. This report is sent to hundreds of thousands of stockholders, brokerage houses, banks, the financial press, the prospective stockholders. As with most large companies' annual reports, this one is a class act.

To conform to SEC standards, financial department heads, executive and finance committees, key officers and directors, legal counsel, and the financial PR staff all have a hand in producing the annual report. The financial staff will then work with design and editorial people and printers on the physical look of the report. It's a long, tedious project with a high budget and high priority. Although quarterly reports are less comprehensive, they are nonetheless important because they give stockholders interim information about the company's progress.

In addition, financial PR people are called upon to produce analyst yearbooks that contain more information than the usual report. They also produce annual-meeting reports documenting a company's growth and direction, corporate annual reviews supplementing the annual report, and summary reports that focus directly on a corporation's financial and operating results.

The publication *Financial World* conducts an annual competition rewarding excellence in corporate annual reports.

OTHER RESPONSIBILITIES OF FINANCIAL PR AND INVESTOR RELATIONS DEPARTMENTS

In addition to preparing the annual report, financial PR people work closely with top executive management on a variety of tasks. They write releases on all financial matters and disseminate this material to all sources. They may be chosen to write the CEO's speech for the annual stockholder's meeting or prepare the presentations by corporate financial officers to groups of security analysts.

Investor relations (IR) people also handle correspondence with stockholders. They consult with the company's advertising departments and advertising agencies on corporate financial advertising. IR staff coordinate their own efforts with that of the company's outside PR counsel, often PR specialists.

Another key activity of IR people is contact with the business press;

that is, trade magazines dealing with the company's corporate and financial issues.

When a company is facing a possible takeover or bankruptcy, IR staffers are part of an in-house and PR counsel team, trained to offer the proper response to this vital concern. IR people also deal with foreign investors, mutual funds and institutions, and the foreign press.

CAREER TIP:
INVESTOR RELATIONS—A GROWTH MARKET

IR is an excellent field for M.B.A.s who have writing and PR training. Opportunities exist at both the corporation and PR counsel firms specializing in financial PR. PRSA has an Investor Relations Section for professionals in this specialty. New York University and UCLA also offer training programs in investor relations. See chapter 19 for the addresses of these resources.

CHAPTER 15

Personal and Entertainment PR

PERSONAL PR

Personal PR is typically the province of "publicists," paid agents who spend much of their time trying to get stories published or broadcast about their clients.

Donald Trump, Rupert Murdoch, Leona Helmsley, Jesse Jackson, Michael Milken, authors, professional athletes, fashion designers, society figures, local and national politicians—all retain publicists to publicize their activities. At times the publicists are even charged with the responsibility of keeping their clients' names *out* of the media. As long as the public maintains its insatiable need to read about celebrities, the publicity mill will continue to pump the information out.

How Professionals Use PR

Public relations for attorneys, physicians, accountants, and other professionals didn't exist twenty years ago, but today these people are using PR and promotion to boost their fortunes. Here are a few techniques that are used:

- Interviews to local media on subjects of interest to consumers
- The writing of op-ed pieces for local newspapers
- Writing and preparing booklets with advice to consumers
- Delivering speeches to local business groups
- Serving as on-air commentator on local TV and radio stations
- Sponsoring seminars on the areas of expertise of the professional
- Issuing periodic newsletters for clients and local media pickup.

ENTERTAINMENT PR

Entertainment PR has existed in the United States for as long as there has been entertainment, predating even P. T. Barnum. When Henry Rogers founded his own PR firm in 1935 with $500 lent to him by his father, there were already three top publicity offices, all run by women.

Those were the days of the powerful Hollywood syndicated columnists Hedda Hopper and Louella Parsons. Breaking into their columns was the ticket to heaven for publicists. Henry Rogers and his partner, Warren Cowan, broke into those columns and many others for a roster of clients that included Joan Crawford, Rita Hayworth, Rosalind Russell, and Olivia de Havilland. By 1965, Rogers and Cowan had become one of the preeminent independent publicity agencies in the entertainment industry and, in the process, had given the field a new respectability.

Under the old Hollywood studio system, the studio was responsible for the publicity of its movies and its contract stars. Once that system was eliminated, the stars engaged their own publicists. This practice exists not only in films but also in TV and the music business.

The entertainment publicity mill churns out information to

hundreds of important media sources that use it to feed the public's insatiable hunger for news of show business luminaries.

Entertainment PR has grown in sophistication since its early days. Publicists of major stars are in power positions. One leading Hollywood press agent, Pat Kingsley, controls access to more than ninety stars, including Julia Roberts, Woody Allen, and Michelle Pfeiffer. Kingsley rejects journalists' requests more often than she accepts them. Her explanation: "It's not our job to give the press everything they want."

Much of entertainment PR involves tie-ins. That is, when you see Bruce Willis, Julia Roberts, and Warren Beatty on the covers of major magazines, more often than not it means that they have a movie in release when the publication goes on sale. The major stars' publicists can decide which magazines are to receive exclusives, select the photographer and writer, and even have a say in the length of the story. There is a great deal of negotiating in this field.

What do entertainment PR people do on a day-to-day basis? Here are a few of their chores:

- arrange for print or broadcast interviews
- set the guidelines for the interviews
- write press releases and send them to the media
- make follow-up telephone calls to the media to encourage stories and interviews
- shepherd clients to appearances
- act as spokesperson for clients, especially regarding controversial matters.

Is entertainment PR a stress-filled occupation? It certainly is. It may also be a rewarding one, as it was for Henry Rogers, who spent fifty years in this pursuit.

AN INTERVIEW WITH A PUBLICIST
AT A LEADING ENTERTAINMENT PR FIRM

John West is a publicist with PMK, Hollywood's most powerful public relations firm. He personally handles such luminaries as Michelle Pfeiffer, Woody Allen, Robert Redford, Liza Minnelli, Barbara Hershey, and Carrie Fisher. We asked John about his craft.

What was your career path on the way to becoming an entertainment publicist?

I had always been fascinated with Hollywood, television, and the movies. It seemed clear to me early on that somehow I would be involved in the entertainment industry. I was raised in San Diego and attended the University of Southern California's School of Cinema and received my B.A. with an emphasis on [film] history and criticism, as opposed to production. Since I longed to live in New York, I applied and was accepted at New York University in their graduate film program, where again I was going to emphasize history and criticism. After my first semester, however, I was eager to work full time, so I left school and began looking for work. A classmate from USC was working for United Artists in New York in their publicity department. He had interned with them during the summer and upon graduation had been offered a full-time job. It was through this friend that I first became aware of publicity and public relations. The more I heard about his job, the more fascinated I became.

I interviewed at most of the studios that had publicity offices in New York, but without success. Finally, through a series of coincidences (a lucky break), I was hired by Bobby Zarem, an independent publicist, who handled all sorts of entertainment accounts. Unfortunately, his office wasn't quite my niche, so I continued looking and found a job with a much larger company, ICPR, that handled both entertainment and corporate accounts. I worked as the assistant to one of the vice presidents and began learning the basics of the business.

After a year or so, the person I was working for moved over to PMK Public Relations and asked if I would go with him as his assistant. Six months after making that move, I was promoted to the position of publicist. I am still with PMK, but have since relocated to Los Angeles.

Movie stars, directors, and even screenwriters have their own publicity counsel. The studios also maintain substantial PR staffs, and on a particular picture, the production engages a unit publicist. What are the functions of each?

A *personal publicist* is hired by an actor, director, screenwriter, producer, or anyone else involved in the entertainment industry to advise on the most effective use of publicity. The client may hire the publicist to oversee just one particular project that he or she wants to draw attention to, or to oversee the client's career on an ongoing basis.

The personal publicist arranges and counsels the client on which interviews to do. Each interview is arranged to serve the client's best interest. When possible, we like to have a say in who will do the interview, who will take the photograph, and how it will be featured in the publication. It is rare to have total control over a situation, but the publicist tries to manipulate the elements to the client's best advantage.

The publicist also advises the client on which personal appearances to make and then makes all the arrangements. This includes award shows, charity benefits, speaking engagements, public service announcements, and so forth.

The *studio publicist* is solely responsible for the studio's roster of films and publicity that concerns the studio on a corporate level.

The studio publicity department oversees all aspects of a film's publicity and promotion from pre-production through production, post-production, and release. This department oversees visits to a movie set by the press, as well as production stories and magazine, newspaper, radio, and television interviews for a film. The studio publicity department arranges screenings of the film for the press, organizes the film's premiere or other event, oversees the still photographs used to publicize the film and the electronic press kit. The electronic press kit (EPK) is a video presentation about a film that may include footage of the film in production, interviews with the producer, director, and stars, and any other relevant information that will be useful to the broadcast media. In addition, the studio publicity department is responsible for the production notes on a film, often with information supplied by the unit publicist. These are handed out to the press to give them background on the film and the creative team behind it.

The *unit publicist* is hired by the production company or the studio to deal with all publicity activities while a film is in production. He or she is likely to be with the film on location on a daily basis.

The unit publicist arranges visits to the set by both the broadcast and print press. It is the unit publicist's responsibility to see that these visits are not disruptive to the production, but still get the job done.

The unit publicist writes the production notes for the film. The notes include information about the evolution of the project, what went on during production with quotes from the creative team, and short biographies of the stars, director, producer, screenwriter, and director of cinematography (and often other behind-the-scenes people). The completed notes are then handed over to the studio.

The unit publicist stays in constant contact with the studio to let it know how things are progressing or if there are any problems that require studio intervention.

The unit publicist is also responsible for ensuring that the actors who have photo approval review all the artwork shot by the film's unit photographer in which they are featured, and then make their "kills."

What are the negative aspects of being an entertainment publicist? About how many phone calls do you make or receive on any given day?

The negative aspects are similar, I'm sure, to those of any other kind of publicist. One deals with a wide variety of personalities both as clients and as members of the press. Obviously, some are more demanding and difficult than others. Also, you often wish that you had more control over how a story turns out, particularly when it doesn't turn out the way you or the client hoped it would.

I probably average about fifty phone calls a day. Some days more, some days less.

Your business is based on relationships. An interview for a star on "The Today Show" is supposed to be worth more than feature stories in the New York Times *and the* Los Angeles Times *put together. How are such appearances arranged? What are the strategies used?*

To arrange any interview, whether print or broadcast, you first begin by calling your contact at the media outlet to sell the story. In television you contact the talent coordinator for a talk show, or the producer for a news or entertainment program. For radio, you contact either the assignment desk for a particular station or radio network, or most often you deal directly with the interviewer. For print interviews, you deal with the appropriate editor at a newspaper or magazine, or often you deal with a freelance writer who has a relationship with the outlet and then have the writer sell the publication on the story.

You need a good working knowledge of the media—what types of television programs, radio programs, newspaper sections, and magazines are out there. Half the battle is pitching the right person the right angle. You have to evaluate either the individual client or the project and decide which idea or angle you have the best chance of selling.

How are satellite press tours organized?

Our office or the studio will often contract this assignment out to a company that specializes in organizing press tours. We work with that company to ensure that the kind of interviews we're looking for are secured.

The idea of a satellite press tour is that the client can sit in a television studio in one city, and via satellite conduct short interviews with television stations across the country. Previously, one would have to travel from city to city. Obviously a satellite press tour is much more convenient. Most of the interviews we look for are on local morning shows ("Good Morning Cleveland," for instance) or local news programs, which usually have a short entertainment section.

In recent years we have seen the introduction of dozens of new TV shows like "Entertainment Tonight" and numerous interview shows focusing on entertainment celebrities. There are also magazines with the same orientation, such as People, Entertainment Weekly, *and* Us. *How have these developments affected the publicity business?*

The recent surge in entertainment-related television programs like "Entertainment Tonight" and magazines like *People, Us,* and *Entertainment Weekly* has provided us with a real boon. The competition among them offers us the opportunity to have more control over a particular interview. If one magazine won't give us the cover, another probably will. Our clients become more in demand because of the number of outlets wanting interviews with them, and we can afford to be more particular—thus keeping the client happy.

The increased coverage of entertainment also means that the media is more apt to do stories on lesser-known figures than they were in the past. They are also more interested in doing features on the behind-the-scenes people (directors, producers, screenwriters, et cetera) than ever before.

It has been reported that your agency represents about ninety clients. How many clients does one agent handle?

PMK Public Relations has both an office in New York and one in Los Angeles. Each coast has approximately eight publicists, and each publicist handles an average of ten to twelve clients at any given time.

Each client is assigned a publicist in Los Angeles and one in New York who keep in constant contact with the client. As most of the media is still based in New York, we find it invaluable to have a presence there as well as in Los Angeles. So often it is the personal relationship with a magazine editor or broadcast producer that will help cement the story assignment.

As the media's interest in entertainment continues to rise, an increasing number of media outlets are now headquartered in Los Angeles. Since most of the studios, television networks, production companies, talent agencies, and most of our clients are based in Los Angeles, we find that the L.A. office is more involved in the "business" end of what we do.

CHAPTER 16

PR for Advocacy and Environmental Organizations

In Washington, D.C., seven blocks apart, are the headquarters of two organizations at opposite ends of the sensitive issue of abortion. The National Abortion Rights Action League (NARAL) is the political arm of the pro-choice movement. It has 34 state affiliates and 300,000 members nationwide. Its basic function is to provide speakers and information about abortion rights.

The National Right to Life Committee represents 50 states and 2,500 local right-to-life groups. Its purpose is to provide educational, political, and lobbying services on issues of abortion, infanticide, and euthanasia.

These two groups are typical of the thousands of advocacy and environmental organizations, many of which are based in Washington. Some of these organizations are citizens' action committees; others are sponsored by business and industry.

Examples of other such groups, along with their statements of purpose, follow.

• Defenders of Wildlife: a national conservation organization protecting wild animals and plants in their natural environment, especially native American endangered or threatened species

• Greenpeace USA: an environmental advocacy group that provides information on pollution, disarmament, and ocean ecology issues

• Humane Farming Association: the nation's leading farm animal issues organization

• SANE/FREEZE: the nation's largest national peace and disarmament organization with 160,000 members.

On the other side of the spectrum are industry groups whose purpose is to disseminate information about business's point of view on various issues. Among these, and their stated purposes:

• American Forest Council: develops public understanding of wood and paper products and their link to a productive forest

• Health Industry Manufacturers Association: provides information on issues such as FDA regulations, Medicare, and health care financing

• National Rifle Association: trains millions in the safe and responsible use of firearms and teaches hunter skills and safety.

HOW INDUSTRY JOINED THE ENVIRONMENTAL BANDWAGON

Susan Schaefer Vandervoort, a PR specialist in environmental issues, calls the new language of environmental problems and solutions "ecospeak" and the groups monitoring industry's participation in these programs "Green Brother."[25]

Public relations professionals are becoming increasingly active on behalf of clients eager to present a positive face to their publics on environmental issues. McDonald's took a major step in proving that it is an environmentally responsible company when it took the initiative in replacing its polystyrene serving materials with more "ecologically friendly" materials.

Procter & Gamble gained national publicity as one of our most environmentally conscious companies for its policy of incorporating recycled plastic in its bottles and for its efforts in developing a more compostable disposable diaper.

Vandervoort emphasizes four principles for companies eager to improve their environmental record:

- Make your environmental policy real
- Get out in front of the issues
- Go beyond compliance
- Communicate your actions

An effective public affairs program, she maintains, must be thoroughly researched, tested, and evaluated.

RESPONSIBILITIES OF PR PEOPLE ON ADVOCACY AND ENVIRONMENTAL CAMPAIGNS

If you work for one of these organizations, what kinds of activities are you involved in on a day-to-day basis? Here are some typical tasks:

- produce literature conveying the aims and purposes of the group
- work on media relations, which includes feeding the press articles on the organization and handling inquiries from the media
- collaborate with industry on events and campaigns promoting the organization
- write speeches for organization leaders
- create and implement direct-mail campaigns
- collaborate with local member groups
- write and edit newsletters
- work on fund-raising campaigns
- coordinate local, national, and international events
- lobby: the primary reason most of these groups are headquartered in Washington. Lobbying attempts to influence legislators on behalf of an organization's point of view on various issues. Many

lobbyists previously worked as congressional aides or with government agencies. Working for environmental and advocacy organizations, they meet with members of Congress, legislative aides, and heads of governmental agencies in order to promote their agendas—a tiring effort, but one that can produce very positive results.

There are more than 200 organized environmental groups in the United States today,[26] the largest being Greenpeace, with 1,800,000 members. Environment and advocacy organizations represent excellent employment opportunities for PR professionals.

**AN INTERVIEW WITH
THE DIRECTOR OF COMMUNICATIONS
FOR A CONGRESSIONAL COMMISSION**

Madalene B. Milano is director of communications for the National Commission to Prevent Infant Mortality, a sixteen-member bipartisan congressional commission. She has been with the commission since May 1991.

Before joining the commission staff, Milano was a senior account executive at The Widmeyer Group, a media relations agency in Washington, D.C. Concentrating on such front-line issues as children, families, and health care, Milano helped design the media strategies that generated national attention for studies and public-awareness projects developed by the National Commission to Prevent Infant Mortality, the National Academy of Sciences, Columbia University School of Public Health, the National Commission on Children, and the Southern Governors' Association's Southern Regional Project on Infant Mortality.

Milano has established herself as a source of information to the journalists and editors who work on health-oriented issues. In addition to regularly placing clients and commission members on top-rated television and radio programs nationwide and throughout the pages of the major dailies, she has generated interest in health- and social-issue stories on such in-depth programs as CBS-TV's "48 Hours," and ABC-TV's "American Agenda" segment and "Nightline."

Her other relevant PR firm experience has included work for such prestigious groups as the Carnegie Council on Adolescent Development, W. T. Grant Foundation, and the American Federation of Teachers.

Milano was born in Bowie, Texas, on November 16, 1963. She received her Bachelor of Science in Journalism from the Perley Issac

Reed School of Journalism, West Virginia University. She lives in Washington, D.C., with her husband, Michael J. Milano.

You have worked on both sides of PR, first with a PR counsel firm and now as a one-person PR staff with a congressional commission. How do these functions differ?

Working for a public relations agency provided me with extensive knowledge of media and public relations techniques and applications. The variety a firm can provide in respect to both the accounts you service and the experience of the people you work with is unique. At the agency I also learned greater time-management skills because of the billable hours routine and honed my "customer relations" skills—the key to this business!

The commission has provided me with ground to use and broaden my agency experience—to "spotlight" my expertise, if you will. I sought internal communications in an effort to "specialize" in children and health issues. The agency did not allow me the time to improve and build on my knowledge of the issues I promoted. By the time I finished one project, I was off on another without much time for follow-up. Many PR professionals thrive on the variety an agency can provide—"PR is PR no matter where you apply it," they say. I, however, need to feel that I *know* what I'm talking about when I'm pitching a story or designing an awareness campaign. So, I'm really much more in "my element" at the commission.

Please describe some of your typical activities at the National Commission to Prevent Infant Mortality.

As director of communications at the National Commission to Prevent Infant Mortality my days are never the same! My main responsibility is to consult the executive director and staff "project directors" on strategies to encourage greater media and public awareness of the infant mortality issue. (We have a professional staff of eight.)

I am an "arm" of each project underway at the commission, providing media consultation as well as technical assistance based on my long-term relationship with the commission and knowledge of the issue. I direct and I am usually the sole staff person on all projects that deal directly with influencing public awareness, i.e., public-service campaigns, etc.

Much of my time is spent answering media requests for information or interviews and soliciting media attention through writing pitch letters for story ideas, op-eds for placement in major newspapers, letters to the editor, and other forms of direct media contact.

I also serve as the primary media liaison with congressional staff both at the federal and state level and as adviser to related organizations and agencies on communicating maternal and child health/education issues.

I am the coordinator for all "breaking news" events. I coordinate the press conferences, briefings, editorial board meetings, and/or one-on-one meetings with media. I write the press advisories, releases, and talking points; create the press kits; and make the media calls to promote the events. We are usually involved in four to five "reactionary" media events per year, i.e., the release of up-to-date infant mortality data by the federal government. We've been very successful in "tapping" our target media for inclusion of our spokespersons in these stories.

My goal at the commission is simple: Never let the issue die down in the public eye. There may be peaks and valleys, but a news hit every four to six weeks keeps us visible and has really paid off in bringing this issue closer to the public and to the policymakers who make things happen.

Media relations involves a great deal of writing. How advantageous was your journalism background in preparation for this job?

I firmly believe that my journalism background is what gets me through this job day-to-day. Learning to write well is important, but the knowledge of how to write for *media*, how media work, their deadlines, what makes a story newsworthy, and when to break a story all lead to greater media and public relations skills. I also gained a greater respect for journalists through journalism school, and this has helped me in building relationships with media throughout my career.

Are salaries substantially lower in a public-policy job than they are in the private sector?

Yes, although I'm not sure because I was able to negotiate my salary coming in from a "higher-than-normal salary" private-sector job, and I built in a salary increase. Let's just say that I know more people in the private sector making good salaries than I do people in the public sector. I really think it's all relative. A lot of people making really good money hate their jobs! Also, I don't equate money with opportunity, and there is a lot of opportunity for experience in the public sector.

What advice can you give to those planning to enter the field of PR?

My advice: internships, internships, internships! In media and public relations, there's nothing to beat practical experience. You can learn only the basics of PR in school. Building technique, strategy, even creativity comes *on the job*. This is a fast-paced, often high-stress field, and there is a lot of competition. You have to be confident in what you know and all that you do, so learning as much as possible before you begin your professional career is important.

CHAPTER 17

Corporate Advertising

C orporate advertising is a form of public relations that calls attention to the company or separates it from its competitors in the eyes of its publics.

Corporate advertising is also used to help solve a problem or ward off a threat by offering the company's views on an issue. It is sometimes called issue advertising, institutional advertising, idea advertising, or advocacy advertising.

A two-page spread in *The New Yorker* for Toyota is a textbook example of excellent corporate advertising. The left-hand page has a picture of the Georgetown, Kentucky, fire chief in his new fire truck. The soft-sell headline on the right-hand page reads, "The MAYOR reckons I'm like A GLASS of warm MILK. I help all of GEORGETOWN get a good night's SLEEP.—Larry Adkins, Georgetown fire chief."

The body copy of the ad goes into the institutional message. Toyota owns a plant in Georgetown that employs 3,200 people, 95 percent of whom are Kentuckians. Toyota pays about $1 million in local taxes, which enables the town to employ a professionally trained fire chief and 10 full-time firefighters. Clearly, Toyota's locating the plant in this town is giving its economy a boost.

For a Japanese automaker with continuous backlash problems, institutional corporate advertising provides positive image building. Interestingly, this series of ads was not prepared by Toyota's regular ad agencies but instead was done by a small New York agency. The ad ran in *The New Yorker* and a number of other upscale, influential magazines. It is an excellent example of advertising that works as public relations.

AT&T has used corporate advertising to promote its support of the arts, and Aetna Insurance has spotlighted its sponsorship of a public TV series, "The American Experience." The Chemical Manufacturers Association ran a series of ads containing warnings about the danger of household chemicals to small children. These ads are excellent examples of the diverse use of corporate advertising.

An ad in *Washington Journalism Review* for the Humane Farming Association is yet another example of corporate or institutional advertising.[27] This ad discusses the sad plight of calves used by factory farms to produce "milk fed" veal. A coupon asks for tax-deductible contributions to promote this cause. The Humane Farming Association places this ad so that journalists seeing it might be inclined to write articles that will bring the association's point of view to the attention of the public.

The American Dairy Association might run an ad to debate the position of the medical community regarding cholesterol levels found in dairy products. The National Livestock and Meat Board might run similar defensive ads.

Sears, Roebuck; Ford; and Chrysler are the three largest corporate advertisers, each spending more than $30 million a year in this specialized area. Network TV gets the biggest share of these dollars, followed by consumer magazines.

Especially in these days of corporate raiding and high-flying mergers and acquisitions activity, corporations consider it necessary to sharpen their images and create greater awareness of their identities.

Why does a corporation invest in corporate advertising? One reason certainly is to stave off attacks from its opponents, be they consumers, regulatory agencies, or competitors. When a company is in a proxy battle for control or takeover, corporate ads are a common defense technique. Similarly, when a corporation faces a crisis—air crash, product contamination, and the like—corporate advertising serves as a valid defense tool, along with public relations.

CHAPTER 18

Crisis Communications

and

Crisis Management

Any of the following situations constitutes a threat to a corporation, organization, government, or governmental agency:

- nuclear accident in an energy plant
- riots and civil unrest
- hostile takeover of a company
- product tampering
- labor–management strife
- filing for bankruptcy
- oil spill
- plant closing and layoffs
- sharply reduced earnings
- fires and major accidents
- insider trading or corporate mismanagement

Some prominent crises we have witnessed in recent times include:

- Los Angeles, April 1992: the looting and arson following the verdict on the Rodney King police brutality trial, causing the deaths of more than 50 people and property loss of more than $750 million
- *Exxon Valdez,* 1989: the oil spill in Alaska that caused massive environmental destruction
- Salman Rushdie's book *The Satanic Verses,* 1989: threats of terrorism by Moslem fundamentalists against a book publisher
- Chernobyl, 1986: the explosion of a nuclear reactor in the former Soviet Union, resulting in many deaths and the spread of radiation throughout Europe
- Bhopal, 1984: the injuries and deaths of thousands from the release of gas in a Union Carbide plant in Bhopal, India
- Tylenol tampering, 1982: the deaths of eight persons in the Chicago area because of the placing of cyanide in Tylenol capsules

When disasters like these strike, an organization must be prepared to institute crisis management. Part of that management consists of communication with the media, stockholders, and the company's various publics.

Companies and institutions with crisis communications programs generally deal with crises as follows[28]:

- a crisis communications team is identified
- the crisis team assesses the situation
- spokespersons, usually people specifically trained in this demanding function, are chosen
- key messages, such as "We will provide the media with updated information as soon as it is available," are identified
- communications methods are determined
- the company rides out the storm

The PR personnel on a crisis team may come from the organization's media relations staff, its PR counsel firm, or both. In a corporation a select group of senior executives heads the team with the CEO as the quarterback calling the signals. The firm's top PR executive and legal counsel serve as the CEO's chief advisers.

According to PR industry leader Jack Modzelewski, the CEO's seat is "closest to the flames, and the CEO ultimately must make the big decisions and then face the public, shareholders, employees, customers, and yes, board of directors to explain the wisdom of these decisions."[29] These actions become more significant when a company is facing a ravenous press.

Not all corporate crises involve accidents or disasters. A company going into bankruptcy needs the good will and understanding of its stakeholders if it hopes to survive. As an example of one company's successful crisis management in a bankruptcy situation, consider the case of Revco.

CASE 1: MANAGING A BANKRUPTCY CRISIS

In July 1988 Revco D.S., a Twinsburg, Ohio–based drugstore chain of 2,000 stores in 27 states, more than 26,000 employees, and sales of $2 billion annually, filed for Chapter 11 bankruptcy.[30] Under Chapter 11, a financially troubled company is allowed to continue doing business under certain conditions and under the dictates of a bankruptcy court and a creditors' committee. Not only does a Chapter 11 company get unfavorable press, but its competitors are quick to spread to suppliers and others word of the company's impending demise.

In legal and financial circles, one refers to the "protection" and "safety" of Chapter 11. Revco D.S. enjoyed little of these safeguards. In fact, soon after the filing, it was hit by an unsolicited takeover offer, the closing of more than 100 stores, media coverage of alleged insider trading in Revco's 1986 leveraged buyout, rumors of inventory shortages, news reports of financial losses, and a decision to downsize the company by selling off 712 stores. At this point Revco wisely enlisted the special services of its longtime independent PR firm, Edward Howard and Company of Cleveland. They came up with a plan that basically sought to reach out to all the company's publics at the right time. The plan had three essential goals:

1. to restore faith in and revitalize the company by retaining the confidence of four key constituencies—employees, customers, vendors, and the news media
2. to enlist the participation of the CEO and senior managers
3. to create messages for each of the four constituencies

Each crisis situation is different. For the Revco bankruptcy, the Howard firm, Revco's independent PR consultants, came up with an approach designed to elicit desired behavior and crafted a set of messages for each of the four constituencies as follows:

AUDIENCE	DESIRED BEHAVIOR	PRIMARY MESSAGE
Employees	Stability—do not quit	Together we can beat this
Customers	Shop at Revco	Business as usual
Vendors	Ship products to us	You'll get paid
Media	Trust us	We will level with you

The execution of the plan called for Revco to:

- Reinforce these messages repeatedly
- Respond immediately to media inquiries
- Publish a weekly employee newsletter
- Update vendors with a newsletter to them
- Set up employee meetings
- Increase CEO accessibility
- Chase down rumors
- Review message content on all press stories on the company.

The results: Revco D.S. survived. Most of its goals were met. Vendors sold merchandise to the company on regular terms. Its credit standing was rebuilt. Most important, Boake Sells, Revco's CEO, won a big gamble. After rejecting an October 1991 offer from the Rite Aid Corporation to buy Revco for $735 million in February 1992, the bankruptcy court approved the company's reorganization statement, allowing the creditors to vote on a $925-million plan that would keep the company independent.

Another significant result: Revco's credibility with the media remained intact. Oh, yes, the Howard company was recipient of the Public Relations Society of America's Best of Silver Anvil Award for best communications effort. The cost of the campaign—about $500,000, and well worth it.

Howard's sixteen-person PR staff is clearly responsible for the winning campaign, but it could not have been won without Revco's dynamic CEO, Boake Sells. At various points he opened his phone line to personal calls from employees. He also visited stores all over the country and introduced himself to customers and employees, inviting them to "Call me Boake." (In an ownership change in 1992, Sells was replaced as CEO.)

This campaign shows PR at its best. Revco illustrates crisis management at a corporation. Consider a crisis of a very different nature.

CASE 2: HOW CRISIS MANAGEMENT WORKED IN A LOCAL DISASTER

On January 17, 1989, a gunman armed with a semiautomatic assault rifle killed five small children and wounded twenty-nine other children and a teacher in a school playground in Stockton, California, then took his own life. The wounded were sent to seven area hospitals, and all but seven children were reunited with their families within hours of the attack.[31]

Investigators were at first baffled by the motive for Patrick Edward Purdy's random shooting of the students despite the discovery that Purdy had been a student at the same elementary school. Later, his attack was analyzed as the result of a long history of anger and emotional disturbance.

The incident, dealing as it did with the controversial subject of semiautomatic weapons, drew national press coverage and soon became a media circus. Managing the crisis was a team of school district administrators led by a cool-headed retired military officer, John Klose, then working as the public-information officer of the school district.

Klose took immediate charge. First, he closed the school to the media. The police agreed that they would handle all questions regarding the crime and that Klose would handle all questions about the school and the children.

The "Today" show, "CBS Morning News," and "Nightline" picked up immediate live coverage. Six satellite trucks and thirteen microwave units were parked in front of the school.

Klose established an almost military routine to the press questioning. The school district received about one hundred media calls a day. Klose took most of them. He allowed only limited access to the teachers, already grief-stricken by the incident, some having held dying children in their arms. Klose had to restrain people from the governor's office who wanted to take over, especially during the memorial service.

An apparently well-intentioned visit of superstar Michael Jackson had to be warded off. Yet more than 1,000 people stormed the elementary school, breaking down barricades, climbing trees and knocking on windows—just to see Jackson. Extra police were called in to control the crowd. Klose himself became a media celebrity. He was lauded for his efforts as an "interloper" in this crisis situation of a local disaster, one with national implications. Later, proposed assault-rifle legislation ultimately supplanted public interest in the assault victims.

Crisis communications and crisis management present great challenges to the PR practitioner. For an incident such as the one in Stockton, one needs the cool-headed decisiveness of a John Klose.

All crises are not resolved as well as the Revco bankruptcy or as commandingly as the Stockton case. But even the more routine ones present a challenge to the PR practitioner.

PART IV

Pursuing a Career in Public Relations

CHAPTER 19

Colleges, Extension Programs, and Summer Institutes

THE SIX REQUISITE SKILLS OF PR

Most PR jobs involve one or more of the following.

1. *Programming:* This involves analyzing problems and opportunities, defining goals and the publics, and recommending and planning activities. It also may include budgeting and assigning duties to other people.

2. *Research and Evaluation:* This includes the gathering of information from management and other sources. Fact gathering is a constant activity of PR people. It is done through interviews and research and may also involve using survey techniques and dealing with firms specializing in and conducting opinion research. The process also concerns the evaluation of this material.

3. *Writing and Editing:* The PR person's tool is the printed word. He or she uses it in reports, news releases, film scripts, speeches, product information, employee publications, and so on. A sound, clear writing style is a must for PR work.

4. *Information:* Disseminating material to media sources and enlisting them in publishing or broadcasting it is a major PR activity.

It requires knowledge of how the media work. It also means getting to the right editor/producer at the right publication/program at the right time.

5. *Production:* The PR practitioner needs a working knowledge of the techniques of art, layout, typography, photography, and desktop publishing.

6. *Speaking:* Face-to-face communication is an essential facet of PR work. This may take the form of writing speeches for others as well as addressing individuals and groups.

EDUCATION AND TRAINING

Any training you undertake at the college, postgraduate, or college extension level should concentrate on developing these six skills.

More than 160 colleges and universities offer a PR sequence or degree program. Of these institutions, 150 have on-campus chapters of PRSA, the Public Relations Society of America. Most PR programs are administered by journalism or mass communications schools or departments. Several of these institutions also offer the opportunity for graduate study in PR. For PR students, the most frequently recommended "minor" area of study is business.

New York University's Summer Institute in PR
If you can afford about $1,500—plus living expenses—we recommend NYU's summer PR program. New York is the media communications capital. It is also the home of the leading PR counsel firms.

The Summer Institute has a faculty of almost sixty leading industry professionals who bring their expertise to play in the three-week program. This faculty is drawn from the evening Certificate Program in PR at the Management Institute of NYU's School of Continuing Education, another fine training source. In addition, numerous special guests are invited to speak, conduct workshops, and act as panelists and judges.

The Summer Institute is a total immersion program, with three weeks of daily lecture, demonstration, field trips, practice, and feedback that guide the students through the history, theory, and techniques of public relations. Students prepare news releases and other PR tools. They make field trips to PR agencies, corporations, and video production facilities. The general approach is to learn by doing.

The highlight of the program is "the simulation"—the drafting and presentation of a PR program proposal in response to a specific problem or opportunity, thus replicating the client/agency relationship. Written and oral team presentations are judged and graded by professionals at the conclusion of the Institute's program.

The PR program is limited to only fifty people. For information, call the Institute's office at (212) 998–7219 or write to:

New York University
School of Continuing Education
Management Institute
48 Cooper Square, Rm. 108
New York, NY 10003

UCLA's PR Program

Readers who live in the Los Angeles area or plan to be there for a period of time should consider the Professional Designation in PR program, conducted evenings by UCLA's Extension Division in association with PRSA's Los Angeles chapter. A Professional Designation Certificate is awarded upon completion of nine three-unit courses, including five required courses and four electives. Industry professionals teach all courses. For information, call (213) 825–0641, or write to:

UCLA Extension
Public Relations Programs
P.O. Box 24901
Los Angeles, CA 90024

Graduate Programs in PR

Many fine graduate programs in public relations are conducted by colleges and universities. Ten colleges grant a doctorate in PR. About twenty-five offer masters' degrees in this discipline.

In a 1991 poll conducted by Marquette University's Department of Advertising and PR, the University of Maryland's graduate program was rated best by the members of PRSA's Educators Section. The University of Florida was ranked second, followed by San Diego State University, Boston University, and San Jose State University. Rounding out the top ten were the University of Texas, Syracuse University, Northwestern University, Ohio State University, and the University of Georgia.

STUDENT ORGANIZATIONS

PRSA's Student Society of America

The PRSA, the preeminent PR organization, directs the Student Society of America (PRSSA) with more than 5,000 members in 160 chapters nationwide. It has emerged in recent years as a national pre-professional organization. Some of its activities are:

- *National Conference:* Each fall, students from various chapters convene in a different city for four days of workshops, lectures, networking, and even fun. Here, too, the students are given an opportunity to meet professionals from all sectors of PR.
- *Professional Connection:* This is PRSA's career referral service, offered free to PRSA's Student Society graduates seeking permanent positions in PR. Members can phone in and learn about nationwide PR job opportunities—their locations, salary ranges, and experience requirements.
- *National Competitions:* There are four separate programs. One is a case-study competition, another deals with writing, a third is the National Gold Key for academic excellence in PR, and a fourth consists of preparing and implementing campaigns for various outside organizations.

In addition, PRSSA supports a scholarship and an internship program. Members also receive *Forum,* its national newsletter, and *SWAP,* a national chapter development newsletter written by PRSSA members. In October 1992, PRSSA's 17th National Conference was held in Kansas City. There, members were served a cornucopia of almost fifty lectures and conferences on such subjects as running a successful campaign, the making of a star, how to get your first job and prepare for the big move up, PR around the globe, PR and environmental concerns, corporate employee communication, and effective video news releases.

PREPARING FOR A JOB IN PR

According to a survey of prospective employers, the ideal applicant for a PR job has[32]:

- a four-year undergraduate degree
- experience with courses in news writing, business, and the social sciences
- an outgoing personality and a willingness to work
- the ability to write well
- work experience in a related field.

CHAPTER 20

Executive Training and Internships

GAINING EXPERIENCE IN PR

It is as difficult getting a job at one of the large PR counsel firms as it is to do so at the top advertising agencies. These firms have their pick of outstanding recent graduates. Yet it is worth trying. Some firms have training programs or internships that are particularly valuable to the beginning PR practitioner.

For people still attending school, internships with PR counsel firms, corporate PR departments, or nonprofit organizations are extremely worthwhile.

The most productive internships are those involving assignments of one or more of the following duties:

- writing, layout, and editing for external or internal publications, promotional material, and brochures
- newsgathering, news-release and feature writing
- research and report writing

- preparing lists of key personnel at local newspapers, magazines, and TV and radio stations
- preparing audio/visual presentations
- helping to arrange or take part in special events
- assisting in fund-raising programs.

Graduates with such internships have an edge in the entry-level job market.

Ruder Finn's Executive Training Program

As we have already seen, Ruder Finn is one of the principal PR counsel firms in the world. Commensurate with this status, the New York office of the firm conducts the largest and most competitive executive training program in the industry. So coveted is the program that Ruder Finn attracts outstanding people with M.B.A.s, Ph.D.s, and degrees in journalism, philosophy, anthropology, science, and literature.

Entry-level employees are rarely hired by the firm without having completed its Executive Training Program. Trainees work full time and are paid at the rate of $300 a week. Graduates who are hired become assistant account executives at a much higher salary. Trainees are assigned to one or two account groups. These include Consumer Marketing, Investor Relations, Financial Services, Healthcare, Food/Lifestyle, Public Affairs, Arts, Research, Visual Technology, Hi-Tech, and Japan Group. There are three Executive Training Programs each year. A special committee reviews written applications and selects those to be interviewed in person or by phone. For further information, call Deidra Degn, Internships Coordinator, at (212) 715–1529 in New York.

The Harold Burson Summer Internship

Burson-Marsteller is one of the largest PR firms, with a staff of more than 2,500 in 50 offices worldwide. Each summer, for a 10-week period, a select group of interns participate in the Harold Burson Summer Internship program. The students are paid for their services during this period.

Participants in the program become involved with three areas. First, each is assigned to work with a particular account team on specific client work. Second, each week interns attend a luncheon meeting at which a Burson-Marsteller executive speaks on such topics as research capabilities, media services, creative techniques, and programming approaches. The lecture series assists the interns with the third segment, a presentation pitching new business to a client. In this case, Burson-Marsteller top management plays the role of the client.

Michele McCollister, a Burson-Marsteller intern in 1989, described her "hands on" training in the program:

> I worked with five other interns to develop a PR plan for a Burson-Marsteller account. Six other interns were assigned to the Nutra-Sweet group project, but our group sought to write to college students from the U.S. and the Soviet Union to communicate for world peace via rock 'n' roll. Our program publicized and encouraged student participation in a 1990 Moscow rock concert.
>
> We formulated the program, designed its packaging, and presented the proposal for critique to four of the agency's top executives. This process was a tremendous learning experience which showed me the big picture of the PR business.
>
> At our weekly luncheons, it was New York pizza or cold cuts shared with a different Burson-Marsteller executive. As the interns discussed our projects and assignments, I gained insight into the workings of a number of the agency's accounts—IBM, FTD florists, Hasbro toys, DuPont fibers, and Owens-Corning Fiberglass.
>
> With the passing weeks we (as interns) had grown in experience, knowledge of the business, and in confidence of our abilities. We were more sophisticated and more informed, and our direction was more focused as we questioned the final speaker. It marked the end of a summer and the beginning of my career.

For more information about this fine program, write to:

Harold Burson Summer Internship
230 Park Avenue South
New York, NY 10003

BRINGING EXPERIENCE FROM OTHER PROFESSIONS

Most of today's senior PR practitioners started in journalism. For the majority with this background, PR work represents a change in career objectives. Journalism may still be a stepping-stone to PR. The experience gained in journalism—writing, personal contact, and other aspects of work in the media—lends itself to jobs in PR.

To a lesser extent, experience in general business, marketing, advertising, and selling is considered useful for PR work. Sometimes work in specialized fields such as finance, engineering, medicine, and public or educational administration can provide valuable background for a PR position within a particular organization.

Outside activities—freelance writing, community organization work, election and fund campaigning, public speaking—are often looked upon favorably as supporting experience.

Turning an Internship into a Job

In May 1990, with a degree in psychology from an Ohio college, Kristen Carneal was ill equipped for a job in PR. With her resumé in hand and a determination to break into the field, she was able to land a spot in the "power intern" program of the Washington, D.C.–based PR firm Manning, Selvage & Lee. When the summer program was over, Carneal worked free part-time for the firm from September 1990 until April 1991, when a job opening occurred. By year's end she had become a full-time assistant account executive at the firm and was on her way to a promising career.

Internships are a great way to break into the field, says Keith Greenberg.[33] Companies learn a great deal about the candidate from this experience. They find it easier to evaluate a student's work rather than try to predict potential through reading a resumé.

CHAPTER 21

The Alphabet Organizations of PR

A number of professional organizations in PR may be helpful to newcomers seeking employment, information, training programs, and internships.

PUBLIC RELATIONS SOCIETY OF AMERICA

The PRSA, headquartered in New York City, is the leading professional organization for PR practitioners, with about 15,000 members. It was chartered in 1947 and has 101 chapters throughout the United States.

A principal service of PRSA to its members is a professional development program. Members can belong to one or more of the Society's professional interest sections, which offer opportunities to explore issues and concerns unique to their fields of specialization. They may also take home study courses prepared by PRSA to learn new techniques and skills in PR. Guidebooks, conferences, seminars, publications, and other materials aid members at every career level in maintaining professional skills and acquiring new ones.

PRSA's Accreditation Program
PRSA also conducts a voluntary program to grant accreditation. The letters "APR" after one's name signify "Accredited in Public Relations" and attest to a professional's competency in the practice of PR. Members may earn this accreditation status after passing written and oral examinations and acquiring at least five years of professional experience.

The Professional Connection
PRSA maintains a telephone job bank that is available to members and nonmembers. Job seekers can dial a special phone number to hear a recording (updated weekly) of available PR positions.

PRSA Research Information Center
PRSA maintains a research center located at its New York offices. The PRSA Research Information Center contains a large collection of PR texts, articles, guidebooks, and other materials, with information available on some 1,000 subjects. Each year the Center answers more than 20,000 requests for information and receives more than 1,000 visitors.

PRSA's National Conferences
In October 1992, PRSA conducted its 45th National Conference in Kansas City. At this conference, hundreds of PR professionals attended seminars, roundtables, and workshops on a variety of PR subjects. As an indication of the diversity of PR, here are some of the topics covered in the 1992 conference:

- Keys to Effective Communications in a Crisis
- Launching New Products

- Making the Most of Trade Shows
- Community Relations
  Organizing Grass-Roots Efforts
  Recruiting, Organizing, and Motivating Volunteers
- When and How to Conduct a Press Conference
- Creative Techniques for Gaining Media Attention
- How to Conduct Communications Audits
- Sports Marketing
- Adding Creativity to Everyday Writing
- PR for Professional Services
- Getting Results: What Research Tells Us About Strategic Planning
- How PR Can Help Boost Employee Morale
- Reaching International Media
- Video PR—The Complete Picture

PRSA's Award Program

Each year PRSA issues its Silver Anvil awards for excellence in PR performance in sixteen categories. Its Bronze Anvil awards honor achievements in film, videocassettes, and audiovisuals. The Gold Anvil award recognizes an individual's contribution to PR, and an Outstanding Educator Award is given to a full-time professor whose teaching skills have advanced PR education.

Following are some of the individual winners and their campaigns in a recent Silver Anvil competition. We first list the campaign, then the sponsor, and finally the PR counsel firm, if any, responsible for the campaign. Note particularly the range of subjects and clients involved.

"The Army Recruiter/School Counselor Relationship Program"
Headquarters, U.S. Army Recruiting Command, Ft. Sheridan, Illinois
Burson-Marsteller, New York

"Star Kist/Heinz 'Dolphin Safe' Program"
Star Kist Seafood Company, Long Beach, California

"Great American Food Fight Against Cancer"
    American Cancer Society, Atlanta, Georgia
    DDB Needham Worldwide, Chicago, Illinois

"Celebrating Peanut Butter's Birthday"
    Peanut Advisory Board, Atlanta, Georgia

"The Ellis Island Immigration Museum"
    Statue of Liberty/Ellis Island Foundation
    GCI Group, New York

"Recycle This"
    The Dow Chemical Company, Midland, Michigan
    Ketchum Public Relations, Washington, D.C.

"Crayola Crayons New ColorLaunch"
    Binney & Smith, Easton, Pennsylvania

"St. Louis Convention Center Sports Complex"
    Civic Progress and the St. Louis NFL Partnership, St.
        Louis, Missouri
    Fleishman-Hillard, Inc., St. Louis, Missouri

"A Spudtacular Harvest for Idaho Potatoes"
    The Idaho Potato Commission, Boise, Idaho
    Creamer Dickson Basford, New York

"Prostate Cancer Awareness Week"
    Schering Laboratories, Kenilworth, New Jersey
    Berson-Marsteller, New York

The Public Relations Student Society of America

We have already written about this outstanding PRSA student program (see chapter 19). The group has more than 5,600 members in 166 chapters on college campuses across the country. An internship program, PRIDE (PR Internships to Develop Expertise), gives qualified PRSSA members the opportunity for at least one internship during their academic careers.

PRSA's headquarters is located at 33 Irving Place, New York, NY 10003. Their phone number is (212) 995-2230.

INTERNATIONAL ASSOCIATION OF BUSINESS COMMUNICATORS

The International Association of Business Communicators (IABC) is a worldwide professional organization based in San Francisco with a branch office in London. It has a membership of 11,000 "communicators" in 35 countries. The use of the word "communicators" is significant. It is in the title of the organization and appears throughout the organization's literature, where you rarely see the words "public relations." Perhaps this is done in the interest of maintaining its distance from PRSA.

In any case, the role of IABC is somewhat similar to that of PRSA, with perhaps a greater emphasis on the career and salary advancement of its members. Here are some of IABC's services:

- Publishes a four-color news magazine, *Communication World.*
- Maintains a membership directory of names and addresses of members, allowing for convenient networking.
- Conducts chapter, district, and international meetings, as well as conferences and seminars.
- Offers members a Jobline and a Professional Development Guide for use in career growth.
- Provides five areas of specialization, called "Councils," geared to a member's job responsibilities. Each Council conducts its own seminars and publishes its own newsletter.
- Organizes more than 60 student chapters at colleges and universities throughout the United States and Canada, with more than 1,000 student members.
- Publishes research literature and special reports.
- Gives awards for excellence in communication.
- Coordinates the activity of its more than 120 chapters.

The chapters also offer special seminars as part of their member services package. For a free booklet, "Business Communication as a Career," write to:

International Association of Business Communicators
1 Hallidie Plaza, Suite 600
San Francisco, CA 94102

THE INSTITUTE FOR PR RESEARCH AND EDUCATION

The Institute for PR Research and Education was first established by a group of senior PR practitioners as the Foundation for PR Research and Education. The name change was effected in January 1989. As with the two previously mentioned membership organizations, the Institute's program and operations are funded by tax-deductible contributions from corporations, foundations, PR counseling firms, and individual PR professionals and educators.

The Institute lists as its main goals:

- to commission and disseminate basic and applied research
- to conduct educational programs, seminars, and related activities with professional and educational organizations
- to obtain and allocate adequate funding for research and education.

In addition to these general programs, the Institute has been active on many fronts. It has conducted and sponsored grants and projects to foster the teaching of PR. A major current effort is a study of the priority research questions in this field, such as how PR rules and practices vary from one type of organization to another, and the primary differences in PR working for the public and the private sector. The Institute is also active in publishing, producing films and video, and giving awards for excellence in the field of PR.

INTERNATIONAL PUBLIC RELATIONS ASSOCIATION

The International Public Relations Association (IPRA) has members in Russia, Poland, Bulgaria, Hungary, and China. IPRA is truly an international organization. It has 1,000 individual members in more than 60 countries worldwide.

IPRA was founded in 1955. Its stated objective is "to help spread, throughout the world, the highest standards of PR practice and to assure a free flow of communication." To be eligible for membership, one must have served for at least five years in a senior PR capacity. The greatest asset for an IPRA member is the opportunity for networking with high-level PR executives throughout the world.

IPRA publishes a number of publications and is involved in organizing professional development seminars twice a year. In addition, IPRA holds a World PR Congress every 3 years. The 1990 seminar, held in Brussels, had more than 200 participants from 36 countries.

The group works closely with the United Nations on such projects as its international contest, "Cartoonists Against Drug Abuse." IPRA is also active in environmental issues, sponsoring programs like the project to arrest the degradation undermining the Alpine ecosystem.

THE PUBLIC AFFAIRS COUNCIL

The Public Affairs Council provides many professional services, including:

• Counseling: advising public affairs executives on professional concerns

• Conferences: these vary widely from technique-oriented workshops on public affairs concerns to sophisticated seminars on political trends and emerging social issues

• Public Affairs Institute: a career enhancement program for corporate public affairs executives

• Newsletters and other publications: a monthly newsletter plus various reports and surveys on public affairs topics

• Videotapes and audiotapes: a variety of these are produced on many public affairs subjects.

Readers interested in the services of the Public Affairs Council should write to:

Public Affairs Council
1019 Nineteenth Street, N.W., Suite 200
Washington, D.C. 20036

WICI

Originating in 1909 as Theta Sigma Phi at the University of Washington, Women in Communications, Inc. (WICI), today is an organization of 12,000 members. Its primary purpose is to promote the advancement of women in all fields of communications.

Here are a few of WICI's activities:

• At the direction of WICI leadership, WICI Public Affairs monitors and supports legislation that fosters equal rights and opportunities for women.

• WICI's annual National Professional Conference brings together the nation's best communications professionals, leaders, and speakers for continuing education and career development.

• WICI's Membership Directory is a resource for establishing contacts and support for those entering the communications field or changing careers.

• WICI's national CLARION Awards recognize excellence in print and broadcast journalism, PR, advertising, and photography.

• WICI's national Job Hotline lists communications positions nationwide, and most local chapters offer job services to members.

• WICI publishes an outstanding quarterly magazine, *The Professional Communicator*.

It also features issues, trends, timely information about communications matters, legislation, membership news, women's issues, First

Amendment and freedom-of-information concerns, and career development materials.

WICI has three categories of membership: Professionals in creative professional communications; Associates, individuals employed in communications less than two years; and Students, those working toward a degree and committed to communications as a career.

For more information about WICI membership and activities, write to:

Women in Communications, Inc.
National Headquarters
2101 Wilson Blvd., Suite 417
Arlington, VA 22201
(703) 528-4000

CHAPTER 22

Important Publications and News Services

Many excellent magazines in the field of PR and dozens of fine newsletters cover every facet of this burgeoning field. There are even five publications whose names begin with "PR." Let's discuss some of them.

PR JOURNAL

PRSA's monthly publication, *PR Journal,* is widely considered the leading monthly business magazine for PR professionals. It features news items, in-depth thought pieces, case histories, how-to articles, and management advice.

Readers considering PR as a career choice would do well to read *PR Journal* regularly. It is available in some libraries. The regular feature "People" notes job shifts and promotions, with the heaviest emphasis going to PR counseling firm people. Significantly, many shifts are made from corporate and association jobs to PR counsel firms.

A subscription to twelve monthly issues of *PR Journal* is $49 a year. Write to:

PR Journal
33 Irving Place
New York, NY 10003-2376

BULLDOG REPORTER

This spunky newsletter tells working stiffs how to be as tenacious as bulldogs in scoring media coverage—or, as PR pros say it, "getting the ink." A regular feature focuses on one publication or network and offers inside tips on who covers what at the publication and what kind of pieces they are looking for. *BR* also does case studies on particularly successful promotions or crisis situations.

BR runs a free classified section and reports on media moves. A subscription to this outstanding newsletter is expensive—$397 for twenty-four issues a year. As a PR educational tool it's a must. Seek out a library that subscribes or find a friend in PR who does. The address is:

Bulldog Reporter
2115 Fourth Street
Berkeley, CA 94710

PR NEWS

A profile of *PR News* is a profile of its dynamic founder, Denny Griswold, "the Grande Dame of PR." Griswold's credits in publishing and PR are groundbreaking. Fifty years ago, when women in publishing were rare, she was the managing editor of *Forbes* magazine and later became the first woman on the editorial staff of *Business Week*.

After a stint as an executive at the Edward L. Bernays PR counseling firm, Griswold launched *PR News* in 1944, during World War II, at a time when PR was in its infancy. The *Guinness Book of World Records* cites *PR News* as "the world's pioneer PR publication."

Denny Griswold's gutsy publishing venture paid off. Today, *PR News* is known as the bible of the field, with readers throughout the United States and ninety-one other countries. It is credited with being the principal chronicler of the profession, providing proven techniques and helping increase management support and understanding for the profession.

In addition, "Special Reports" are published on timely, important subjects. These have included "Conversations with 10 Experts in PR," "Handling Crises," "The Outstanding PR Case Studies of the Year," and "The Anniversary as a PR Tool."

Alas, a subscription for fifty-two weekly issues of *PR News* is expensive—$297 per year, a fair price for a PR practitioner, but not for a neophyte.

Try to find it in a good library. The address:

PR News
Phillips Business International
7811 Montrose Rd.
Potomac, MD 20854

IABC'S *COMMUNICATION WORLD*

Just as the International Association of Business Communicators is a competitive organization to the Public Relations Society of America, so is *Communication World* a competitor to PRSA's *PR Journal*. Published eleven times a year, *Communication World* is a slick, informative magazine providing information about the profession of organizational communication.

In addition to feature articles, *Communication World*'s editorial package includes regular departments and columns. Although IABC members receive *Communication World* free as part of their membership, a year's subscription for nonmembers is $48. This subscription is limited to libraries and educational institutions. The address:

IABC
One Hallidie Plaza, Suite 600
San Francisco, CA 94102

inside PR

inside PR is an excellent monthly publication. Each issue contains special departments covering Health and Medicine PR, Public Affairs, Investor Relations, International PR, the Environment, Food and Beverage PR, and a What's New section. The focus of *inside PR*'s editorial coverage is how PR people create measurable results.

The publication has a circulation of 28,000. The subscription price is $50 a year. Their address:

inside PR
235 West 48th Street, #34A
New York, NY 10036

PR reporter

Yet another weekly newsletter of PR, public affairs, and communication for professionals in these fields is *PR reporter*. A highlight of *PR reporter*'s editorial thrust is its in-depth case studies in which the editors interpret a situation and the strategy chosen, the tactics employed, and the results of a PR campaign.

Other features include current issues and trends and their implications and significant news and research results. In addition, subscribers receive weekly supplements.

A subscription to *PR reporter* is $175 a year. The address:

PR reporter
Dudley House
P.O. Box 600
Exeter, NH 03833

PR Quarterly

Newsletter publishing has become a profitable business. There are newsletters for every field of interest, and about 4,000 of them are sold on a subscription basis. The company in Rhinebeck, New York, that publishes the *Newsletter on Newsletters* also publishes *PR Quarterly,* a newsletter presenting an authoritative, practical viewpoint of the PR professions and geared to professionals in this field.

A yearly subscription is $40. For information on *PR Quarterly* write to:

PR Quarterly
P.O. Box 311
Rhinebeck, NY 12572

PR NEWSWIRE

Today, more than 15,000 news sources use PR Newswire every year to send nearly 100,000 messages to media and investors around the world. By accessing the world's largest press telecommunications network, it reaches the people it needs by satellite, fax, mail, and database. A database, or media database, is a computerized directory of individuals and departments within the media to whom publicity solicitations and releases are to be sent.

For financial news releases and information, PR Newswire reaches more than 1,500 newsrooms across the United States. In addition, it provides special distribution of financial news to thousands of offices at brokerage firms, to money managers, and to institutional investors.

PR Newswire does not confine its efforts to financial news. Its circuits process such diverse information as invitations to a press conference, first reports of a major disaster, announcement of a scientific breakthrough, and even a race result as it happens.

In addition to PR Newswire's exclusive national and local news-lines, it extends its electronic reach by offering other newslines such as Public Affairs NewsLine and a dedicated circuit—that is, one set aside for an exclusive or particular purpose, delivering news from the entertainment industry directly to entertainment editors.

CHAPTER 23

The Job Search

FINDING THE FIRST JOB

No task is harder than finding a job, particularly your first. Success in this endeavor requires planning, preparation, energy, and enthusiasm—all in large quantities. Here is some advice from the friendly people at PRSA:

• Research the field in which you have the greatest interest. Use libraries. Journalists are also useful sources.

• Prepare a good resumé. Check and recheck for typographical errors.

• Learn about possible job openings in advance of contacting employers. Scan the list of *Fortune 500* companies. Chances are that these companies have large PR departments. Write to the top PR executive as well as the head of human resources. Follow up your letter with a telephone call.

• Use personal contacts. They are your best sources for job leads, and personal referrals are most advantageous.

• Use business directories for leads and company names. Two

important ones are *O'Dwyer's Directory of PR Firms* and *O'Dwyer's Directory of Corporate Communications.*

• Prepare for an interview by learning as much as you can about the corporations or organizations you are visiting. Read their annual reports and look for articles about them in trade journals.

• Show samples of any press releases you have written and include copies of any press coverage these releases have generated. Your portfolio should contain as well any other writing you have done, particularly if it has been published. Writing for college publications can be used, but only if it is your best effort and is clear, concise, and informative.

• Take the initiative in the interview by describing your qualifications and what you believe you can accomplish on the job.

• Don't fret about rejection; it is no cause to suppose that you will not qualify elsewhere. Consider your job hunt as a learning experience. Perseverance will win you the opportunity to begin your PR career.

• Read any current books you can find about public relations and its related fields.

• Contact your college's alumni association. This will enable you to track people from your school who have gone to work at a company in which you are interested.

• Attend job fairs in which PR firms are participating. Ask specific questions about hiring procedures and company policies.

• Make sure you are adept at cold calling, letter writing, and networking, since these are the ways you will probably get your first job.

• Don't lie or exaggerate on your resumé. Your prospective employer will undoubtedly check references, education, and job experience.

TIPS FROM INDUSTRY PROFESSIONALS

The Public Relations Student Society of America (PRSSA) asked a group of seasoned professionals what they valued in people seeking to break into the field. Their answers offer insight into the experience and characteristics needed to get started in PR.

IF I WERE PLANNING TO ENTER THE FIELD AGAIN TODAY, I'D:

"earn an advanced degree, perhaps an M.B.A. [and] learn more about the social sciences";

"improve my writing skills and learn more about business";

"study liberal arts and work in the college PR office";

"study economics, history, sociology. As vacation preparation I'd get a job on a daily newspaper or a business news magazine";

"see about a foreign job in PR in Hong Kong, London, or Geneva, then return to the U.S. in a year or two";

"get a few years' writing experience in print or broadcast";

"join a counseling firm in any capacity whatsoever";

"study economics and speech, force myself to join debating groups, etc.";

"have a better understanding of techniques of writing and a broader knowledge of report writing."

WHEN INTERVIEWING AN ENTRY-LEVEL CANDIDATE, WHAT IMPRESSES ME MOST IS:

"personal attributes such as appearance, self-confidence, courtesy . . . ability to learn as well as respond thoughtfully . . . how well candidate has done homework about our company, etc.";

"articulateness, clear thinking, pleasant disposition, high energy, and good writing samples that stress ability to think, not just to string words together";

"their knowledge of my company";

"enthusiasm (but not phony), writing ability";

"self-confidence, knowledge of the humanities, interest in business";

"sincerity . . . the candidate's desire to learn from the bottom up";

"breadth of interests—economic, political, social, philosophic";

"ability to manage time";

"brainpower and intellect";

"enthusiasm . . . candor . . . good work samples";

"working experience in media or PR he or she had while
in school";

"crystal-clear and orderly speech—suggesting an orderly
mind";

"ability to listen, as well as converse . . . demeanor and
dress";

"the gray matter he/she has, an eagerness to learn";

"the questions he/she asks";

"evidence of intelligence, motivation, and interpersonal
skills";

"knowledge of what PR is and isn't";

"the preparation the candidates have made for the
interviews."

FINDING A JOB IN HARD TIMES

Getting a job any time is difficult. When times are bad and companies
are downsizing—or even worse, going out of business—finding a job
in PR is a Promethean task. In addition to applying all the tips just
suggested, here is some additional advice that may help the cause:

• Beware of phony employment agents who promise jobs but
really can't deliver. If there is any doubt, check these agents out
through PRSA. Only a small handful of executive recruiters specialize in PR and the media industry.

• Two such companies are Placement Associates, Inc., 80 Fifth
Avenue, New York, NY 10011 and The Howard Sloan Koller
Group, 545 Fifth Avenue, New York, NY 10017.

• Focus on all the major PR companies mentioned in this book.
There is always a better chance of getting a job with a large company than with a small one. The large ones also have their own
training programs and educational benefits.

• Read all the industry trade publications. They not only have
valuable information about PR but often have "help wanted"
columns.

Bob Hart, a managing associate at Foster Partners, a New York
firm that specializes in career counseling, offers this advice for job
hunters:

• Respond to newspaper advertisements, be willing to relocate, follow up on leads from search firms, and organize a letter campaign to potential employers.

• Do not show dissatisfaction with the interview itself. Make it as productive as possible and evaluate it afterward.

• Do not plead for a position.

• Do not discount what executive search companies or human resource departments may be able to do for you.

WRITING A RESUMÉ THAT ATTRACTS ATTENTION

A good resumé should sell *you*. It should clearly state what you bring "to the party." Be career-specific and include the exact dates you held any interim employment. See the sample on page 164 as a good example of an entry-level resumé. It exudes confidence, energy, and leadership.

If you've won any awards for educational excellence or leadership, detail them. Also, list your computer competence, even if most graduates know how to use a personal computer.

Make certain that your resumé is typed or typeset perfectly. If you have writing ability, be prepared to show samples. PR lives on writing. Finally, send a short covering letter with your resumé and say just what you want—an interview.

FINANCIAL WRITING—AN OPEN DOOR

There is a conspicuous need for qualified people in financial PR, particularly those who can write. Writing talent is used in preparing annual reports for companies and financial newsletters for mutual funds and brokerage houses. If you have an M.B.A. and can write, you're way ahead of the pack. Here are a few tips on breaking into this field:

• Large companies such as those in the *Fortune 500* maintain large financial PR staffs. These organizations are your best best for employment.

SUSANNA J. PITT
330 Palmetto Street
Anytown, CA 00000
(714) 555-1234

OBJECTIVE: To obtain employment with a public relations counsel firm, a corporation, or other organization, allowing me to use my communications and writing skills.

EDUCATION: B.A. Management and Communications, University of California at Los Angeles, May 1991. Courses in Marketing Principles, Computer Programming, Graphic Arts, Writing for the Media, Administrative Theory, and Public Relations. Edward R. Tyler Award for Excellence in Public Relations.

Summer Institute in Public Relations, New York University, June 1991. Intensive three-week training program in the fundamentals of public relations, skills development, and the presentation of a simulated public relations program proposal.

UCLA Extension Public Relations Program, 1991. Completed courses in Advanced Writing for Public Relations and Effective Public Relations in the Non-profit Setting.

EXPERIENCE: *Wright-Stevens Public Relations:* Los Angeles, CA.
Assistant Account Executive, July 1991–
Perform all staff duties, including negotiating with editors and broadcasters to produce media exposure for clients. Set up interviews and conduct various kinds of research. Write press releases. Produce collateral material and arrange speaking engagements.

Robinson PR Worldwide: San Francisco, CA.
Paid internship. Assistant Account Executive, May through August 1990.
Aided the account executive in writing and preparing press releases, media kits, and new-product information. Tasks involved writing and media relations. Attended client meetings and presentations.

Professional references available.

• Many PR counseling firms specialize in financial PR. Some of the very large firms have separate financial PR divisions. Check *O'Dwyer's Directory of PR Firms* for a breakdown of 1,800 of these firms and their accounts and branch offices. *O'Dwyer's Directory of Corporate Communications* identifies the individuals heading the financial PR and communications departments at more than 5,300 companies, trade associations, and government bodies.

• If you have a PR job and it is not against company policy to do so, take advantage of the opportunities for freelance work in this field. A typical assignment might be the writing of an investor newsletter for a small brokerage house.

• If you lack a financial and investment background, consider taking extension courses in this specialization at a local college.

• Try to get an interview with a newspaper or magazine financial writer. This person may have many tips and leads on how to get started in this field.

• Read everything you can about investment and finance. Take extension courses on these subjects. Study some of the excellent writing done in this area, such as the feature stories in the *Wall Street Journal* or the work of syndicated financial columnists like Allan Sloan. All this research is good preparation for a job.

AN INTERVIEW WITH
A YOUNG PR PROFESSIONAL

At the age of twenty-eight, Brigitte Devine is already well on her way to success in PR, having entered the field right out of college. We asked her about her background and some specific questions about her present job.

Tell us something about your background.

I was born in Sydney, Australia, in 1964. During the first fifteen years of my life I lived in Madrid, Manila, and Santa Barbara, California, where I attended high school. I began college at the University of California at Santa Barbara majoring in liberal arts, but took a year off to travel to Australia, Asia, and Europe.

While saving money for travel, I gained valuable journalism experience working for a campus newspaper at Santa Barbara City College. After my year of travel, I enrolled at the University of California at Berkeley to study dramatic art and journalism and graduated in 1988 with a degree in dramatic art. I worked my way through all of my years at college. One of my more interesting jobs was an internship at a radio station in Santa Barbara where my memorable first reporting assignment was to interview members of the Hell's Angels on the proposed mandatory helmet law.

Upon leaving Berkeley, I got a job in Los Angeles working for the Harry Winston jewelry company as a production assistant. One of our PR stunts involved the design of a $22 million slice of diamond cake in honor of Beverly Hills's 75th anniversary. My responsibility was to produce two minutes on stage where we had an undercover SWAT team, an armored vehicle, two police cars, and four motorcycle police.

I also hired and costumed actors who presented the cake to Douglas Fairbanks Jr. and Dinah Shore. The most special part of the event was meeting Jimmy Stewart, whom I provided with the prop lighter for the birthday candle.

Through the Winston job I met their New York–based PR firm, Burnham-Callaghan & Associates, and went to work for them in L.A., where I handled such clients as Joel Grey, Hydrotone (a water-based exercise program), and, of course, Harry Winston. After a year, I moved to New York with the same firm, where my clients were a husband–wife drive-time deejay team, two cabaret singers, and a sportswear manufacturer.

Nine months after my arrival in New York, I landed the job of director of PR and advertising at the Harry Winston company, where I have just completed my first year.

What was your major at college, did it help to get your first job, and has it been relevant to your work in PR?

My major in college was dramatic art, with lots of coursework in journalism. The two have certainly given me useful background in my work in public relations, as I have a real appreciation for what the press needs from me—compliance with the deadline and accurate captions. With my first publicity work—representing Joel Grey's "Cabaret" on a nine-month national bus and truck tour—I found myself in the corner in which dramatic art and journalism meet.

You made the change from work at a west coast PR firm to client work with a glamorous company in New York. What are the basic differences between the two jobs?

I find that public relations work is quite different here in New York in that altogether too often the California publicist considers himself to be the celebrity. I have found New Yorkers to be much more straight-forward and grounded, and hence more pleasant to work with. I suppose my job as director of public relations for Harry Winston is glamorous in that I travel quite often, plan and host exquisite parties, and meet very interesting people. But everything has its drawbacks—I cannot have a cat because I'm away so often, and I recently assured my father that if I was learning anything about party planning, it was that he can be assured that if and when the day comes, I'll elope! As for the people—I'll never tire of meeting interesting people.

To what extent are you personally involved in media relations, and how do you interact with your company's public relations firm?

Regardless of whether press relations are initiated by me, our New York press agency, or my counterparts in Europe and Japan, I always become the point person. I personally greet each visiting journalist, give them a tour of our building (where the jewelry is designed and crafted), and follow up with photographs and interviews relative to their needs.

A large part of my job also includes working with fashion editors and stylists who want to use our jewelry in their editorial work. Obviously this is great—and free—exposure for us, so I go out of my way to work with them by offering suggestions per their themes and coordinating transportation and security for the photo sittings.

You do many special events. Describe a typical one, emphasizing your own participation.

My special events consist of two types: those held in the salon, and those held out of the salon, be it in New York or anywhere in the United States. An example of a cocktail reception in our salon is the one we hosted in honor of the New York City Ballet benefit gala committee members last fall. In preparation, I met with the NYCB chairwomen to discuss dates, guest lists, et cetera. From there I took over, ordering invitations, mailing them, coordinating the caterer, florist, photographer. For this particular event, we displayed some of the original costumes from Balanchine's "Diamonds" with our jewelry.

Internally, this meant alerting the sales staff, security, and maintenance, as alarm-rigged furniture had to be removed and additional security put to service. With regard to press, I sent personal invitations to a particular group of journalists, supervised the mailing of a blanket release about the event, then co-wrote items to local society columnists. During the actual event it was my job to act as hostess, greeting guests and helping with photo setups. After the event I wrote captions for the photographs and sent them out and, finally, tallied invoices and drafted a follow-up expense report for accounting purposes.

How large is your staff, and how do they function on a day-to-day basis?
My staff!? Me, myself, and I. Actually I have just been given approval to hire an assistant. Yesterday was her first day, and I'm thrilled—it's going to be a whole new ballgame.

CHAPTER 24

What's Ahead for PR

It is essential to know how the practice of public relations will change in the coming decade. Clearly, globalization is a major trend, as is technological development. The environment is a pervasive public issue facing the business community. The role of minorities, the elimination of stereotypes, and the new demographic realities must be reevaluated. PR faces these and other exciting challenges in the years ahead.

HOW DOES GLOBALIZATION AFFECT PR?

Globalization changes the way multinational companies carry out their PR function. One California-based multinational company, National Semiconductor, one of the world's largest suppliers of semiconductors, has regional communications teams in Japan, Hong Kong, and Germany. It publishes a customer newspaper in these countries. Announcements about new products or new technologies are made through simultaneous press tours in Europe, Southeast Asia, Japan, and the United States, or through a simultaneous satellite transmission.

How can people prepare themselves for today's practice of global communications and PR? Again, we emphasize the need for bilingual and even multilingual PR professionals. PR practitioners must familiarize themselves with the tools to do business globally.

THE GREENING OF PUBLIC RELATIONS

PR people in government and industry address environmental concerns every day. It is one thing, of course, to face the challenges of a crisis such as the *Exxon Valdez* oil spill, but another to present a positive stance on a corporation's environmental record. Presenting a positive position on the environment is clearly why so many companies participate in programs such as Earth Day.

According to one industry commentator, as long as public concern about the environment remains strong, there is a bright future for consultants who are well versed in environmental issues. PR people in this decade must be aware of all environmental considerations and must be prepared to interpret their clients' positions to the public.

VIDEO AS A PR TOOL

The dissemination of PR messages through television is an accepted management tool. The Boeing Company, for example, produced a sixteen-minute video to convey to its employees its new policy on drugs and alcohol. In the video, an employee, in an emotional plea to her fellow workers, recounted her personal battle with drugs. The company's aim is clear: "If you have a drug problem, we want to help you."

Videos are being used to turn out sales promotion motivational films. They are used in stockholder meetings and as a means to tell the company's financial story to security analysts. The use of corporate videos is so widespread that there is even a trade publication covering this field, *Corporate Video Decisions.*

How does the development of video as a PR tool fit into the plans of future PR people? It creates a demand for visually literate specialists—producers, writers, directors, and editors. The preeminent PR organization, PRSA, supports this field by conducting an annual film/video festival. Colleges with PR programs participate actively in this event.

PARLEZ-VOUS RUSSKI?

If you are still in school, add Russian 101 to your PR courses. If you're not, take an extension course in Russian, Japanese, French, Spanish, Italian, German, or Chinese. Doing so will definitely improve your chances of making it in PR.

"I think we're finding more of the people who want to be in the PR business are multilingual," says Peter G. Osgood, vice chairman of Hill and Knowlton. "We look for people who have a second language. It's definitely a benefit."

According to a recent article in *PR Journal,* of 250 PR practitioners surveyed by the International Association of Business Communicators, 30 percent indicated that they are fluent in more than one language.[34]

Seventy-five people in Burson-Marsteller's U.S. offices speak at least two languages. The staff of the firm's European offices are 99 percent bilingual, with more than half speaking at least three languages.

Knowledge of a second language is important for another reason. It shows foreign clients a corporate interest in their culture, which often translates into an advantage.

"Russians, for example, really appreciate anyone who can even attempt to speak their language. To them it's an indication that you are interested in their country," says Paul Brandus at Hill and Knowlton's Washington office.

Taki Andriadis, who speaks seven languages and recently retired from DuPont as intercultural relations vice president, sums it up:

"What U.S. corporations are lacking is the international thinking, the global thinking. And to do this, you have to understand the culture *and* the languages."

More than 100 languages are spoken in southern California, including a dozen Asian languages. U.S. companies are faced with the task of communicating with millions of consumers who don't speak English. Southern California Edison, in the interest of serving its one million Hispanic, 100,000 Asian, and other ethnic groups who don't speak English, has set up a multilingual speakers' bureau. Employees of this bureau conduct special programs and presentations in the language of their customers. This is certainly a sign of things to come in marketing and PR.

NOTES

Chapter 2. PR: What It Is, What It Does

1. Philip Lesly, *Lesly's PR Handbook* (Worthington, OH: Publishing Horizons, 1983).
2. John F. Budd, Jr., "When Less Is More," *Public Relations Quarterly,* Spring 1990, p. 5.
3. *Crain's New York Business,* March 23, 1992.

Chapter 3. The Components of PR

4. Philip J. Webster, "What's the Bottom Line?" *PR Journal,* February 1990, p. 18.
5. Bill Cantor, *Experts in Action: Inside Public Relations* (White Plains, NY: Longman, 1989).

Chapter 6. How PR Works at a Giant Multinational Corporation

6. "IBM Is on Rebound with Streamlined Operations," from Associated Press, *Los Angeles Times,* December 31, 1990, p. D4.

Chapter 7. How PR Works at Other Organizations

7. Sunshine Janda, "Not-for-Profits: A New Ballgame," *PR Journal*, January 1990, p. 22.

Chapter 8. Media Placement and Media Relations

8. American Association of Advertising Agencies, *What Every Account Executive Should Know about Public Relations*, 1989.

9. Lesly, op. cit.

10. Joel Pomerantz, "The Media and PR: Pride and Prejudice," *PR Quarterly*, Winter 1989–90, p. 13.

11. American Association of Advertising Agencies, op. cit.

12. *ABA Newswire*, April 27, 1992, p. 4

Chapter 9. Employee Publications and Employee Relations

13. Alvie T. Smith, *Innovative Employee Communication: New Approaches to Improving Trust, Teamwork and Performance* (New York: Prentice-Hall, 1991).

Chapter 10. Speechwriting

14. "Briefings" column in *Public Relations Journal*, February 1990, p. 12.

15. Advertising supplement in *Public Relations Journal*, January 1991.

16. Timothy J. Koranda, "Writing Speeches with Impact," *Public Relations Journal*, September 1990, p. 31.

Chapter 11. Issues Management and Public Affairs

17. Rayna Skolnik, "Arts and Cultural Organizations Seek Increased Private Support As Public Funding Dwindles," *Public Relations Journal*, February 1992, p. 18.

18. Ernest and Elizabeth Wattenberg, *How to Win in Washington: Very Practical Advice about Lobbying, the Grassroots, and the Media* (Cambridge, MA: Basil Blackwell, Inc., 1990).

Chapter 12. Public Interest, Public Service, Image Building

19. Advertisement in *Washington Journalism Review*, Jan./Feb. 1990.

Chapter 13. Strategic Corporate PR and Integrated Communications

20. Paul S. Forbes, "Applying Strategic Management to Public Relations," *Public Relations Journal*, March 1992, p. 32.

21. Don Hyman, "Pharmaceuticals" Balancing the Demands of Diverse Publics," *Public Relations Journal*, October 1990, p. 22.

22. James Foster, "Working Together," *Public Relations Journal*, September 1990, p. 18.
23. Bennett S. Rubin, "Campaign Opens Door to Safety Issue," *Public Relations Journal*, February 1991, p. 28.

Chapter 14. Financial PR
24. Dennis Connors, "Designing Messages," *Public Relations Journal*, October 1991, p. 15.

Chapter 16. PR for Advocacy and Environmental Organizations
25. Susan Schaefer Vandervoort, "Big Green Brother Is Watching," *Public Relations Journal*, April 1991, p. 14.
26. James T. Harris, "Working with Environment Groups, *Public Relations Journal*, May 1992, p. 24.

Chapter 17. Corporate Advertising
27. *Washington Journalism Review*, July/August 1990, p. 17.

Chapter 18. Crisis Communications and Crisis Management
28. Jonathan Bernstein, "The Ten Steps of Crisis Communications," *The Spectrum*, July 1990.
29. Jack Modzelewski, "What I Would Do," *PR Quarterly*, Spring 1990, p. 12.
30. This account is based on an article edited by Adam Shell in *Public Relations Journal*, September 1990, p. 8.
31. This account is based on an article by William Briggs, "Intercepting Interlopers," in *Public Relations Journal*, February 1990, p. 40.

Chapter 19. College, Extension Programs, and Summer Institutes
32. Dr. Dennis Wilcox, Survey of West Coast Employers.

Chapter 20. Executive Training and Internships
33. Keith Greenberg, "Student interns get real-life experience and sometimes a job," *Public Relations Journal*, December 1991, p. 7.

Chapter 24. What's Ahead for PR
34. "Briefings" column in *Public Relations Journal*, September 1990.

GLOSSARY

Ad/Pub: in the movie and entertainment business, refers to the department responsible for advertising, promoting, and publicizing a film or theatrical production.

Advisory: an announcement or notice that serves to advise the media of the holding of a press conference. May also be used as a guide for securing media credentials for an event.

Angle: also know as slant, peg, or hook. It relates to the point of view from which a release or news story is written, to interest a particular audience.

APR: a title conferred by PRSA, the Public Relations Society of America, designating that the individual is "Accredited in Public Relations," in having completed written and oral examinations and served at least five years in this field.

Backgrounder: a briefing or report for the purpose of providing background information on a governmental agency, organization, or corporation.

Beat: the particular news source or activity covered by a reporter or correspondent in the media.

Clip book: a collection of stories in the media about a client. Usually maintained by a PR firm.

Crisis communications and management: the function of PR when disaster strikes to assess quickly the situation and the damage, assemble all the facts and background information, and offer them to the news media, along with answers to their questions of fact.

Daybook: a listing of upcoming newsmaking events fed by wire services, such as AP and UPI, to broadcasters and other media. PR people feed the events and items to the wire services.

Electronic media monitoring: used by PR people to monitor TV, radio, and wire services coverage. This service is often provided by the same companies that monitor press clippings from print media.

Exclusive: a piece of news sent to a newspaper or other medium, along with the privilege of using it first.

Fact sheet: a listing or statement of details about an individual or group, often included in the press kit sent to the media.

Integrated communications: public relations, advertising, direct marketing, promotion, and other disciplines coordinated through a single planning system.

Media database: a computerized directory of individuals and departments within the media to whom publicity solicitations are made.

Media relations: the vital function of public relations dealing with the preparation and identification of news and information for use in the press and other media.

Pitch: an oral or written solicitation by a PR person on behalf of a story or event.

Placement: the acceptance and appearance of a news item, feature story, or other release in a newspaper, magazine, or broadcast medium. Also relates to "getting ink."

PR firm or counsel: an organization retained by a corporation, organization, or individual to assist its clients in marshaling public relations and public affairs resources. In this respect, it is involved in both planning and execution.

Press agent: a term often used negatively in public relations to refer to individuals whose approach is solely to gain favorable publicity or media attention in almost any way possible. Used frequently in the entertainment industry.

Publics: the entities whose attention is sought by a corporation, individual, governmental agency, charitable organization, and others.

Spokesperson: a person designated to speak for another or for a group.

Strategic communications: the focusing and directing of a corporation's or organization's public relations and marketing plans involving its internal problems, future opportunities, customer concerns, employee relations, and public opinion.

Talking points: facts, features, or short sentences that sum up an organization's position on the issues. Used often by a spokesperson in accenting or highlighting an issue.

Video news release (VNR): a news release transmitted to TV stations via satellite or videotape.

RECOMMENDED READING

Cantor, Bill. *Experts in Action.* New York: Longman, 1989.

Cutlip, Scott M. *Effective Public Relations.* Englewood Cliffs, NJ: Prentice-Hall, 1985.

Goodwin, Richard. *Remembering America.* Boston: Little, Brown, 1988.

Grunig, James E., and Todd Hunt. *Managing Public Relations.* New York: Holt, Rinehart and Winston, 1984.

Lesly, Philip, ed. *Lesly's Handbook of PR.* Fourth Edition. Chicago: Probus Publishing Co., 1991.

Newsom, Doug, and Bob Carrell. *PR Writing: Form and Style.* Belmont, CA: Wadsworth, 1986.

Newsom, Doug, et al. *This Is PR: The Realities of PR.* Belmont, CA: Wadsworth, 1989.

Nolte, Lawrence W., and Dennis L. Wilcox. *Fundamentals of Public Relations.* Elmsford, NY: Pergamon, 1979.

Noonan, Peggy. *What I Saw at the Revolution.* New York: Ivy Books, 1991.

O'Dwyer, J. R. Co., Inc. staff. *O'Dwyer's Directory of Public Relations Firms.* New York: J. R. O'Dwyer, published annually.

Public Relations Career Directory. Hawthorne, NJ: The Career Press, 1988.

Wilcox, Dennis L., Phillip H. Ault, and Warren K. Agee. *Public Relations: Strategies and Tactics,* Second Edition. New York: Harper & Row, 1989.

Wilcox, Dennis L., and Lawrence W. Nolte. *Public Relations Writing and Media Techniques.* New York: Harper & Row, 1990.

INDEX

(Delta)

800-221-1212

10:00
1:00 — $21.00
1:35

4432

2101 725 766